How to
Inspect a House

How to Inspect a House

Exactly What to Look for Before You Buy

George Hoffman

ADDISON-WESLEY PUBLISHING COMPANY, INC.
*Reading, Massachusetts • Menlo Park, California • Don Mills,
Ontario • Wokingham, England • Amsterdam • Sydney
Singapore • Tokyo • Madrid • Bogotá • Santiago
San Juan*

Library of Congress Cataloging in Publication Data

Hoffman, George Cleborn, 1916–
  How to inspect a house.

  Bibliography: p.
  Includes index.
  1. Dwellings—Inspection.   2. House buying.
  I.Title.
  TH4817.5.H64   1985   643'.12   85-1431
  ISBN 0-201-11072-5

A Note to Readers: The author and publisher have made every effort to make sure that the information in this book ensures safety. Because the specifics of each house, environment, and materials vary greatly, the author or the publisher cannot be held responsible for injuries which may result from use of this book.

Text revision by Steve Horgan
Cover design by Marshall Henrichs
Text design by Joyce Weston
Set in 11 point Baskerville by Compset, Inc., Beverly, MA

ISBN 0-201-11072-5

    DEFGHIJ-AL-86
Fourth Printing, February 1986

Dedicated to the people who live in slopey but stable houses, who have learned to serve plates with the vegetables up, the gravy down.

Contents

vii

viii   *Contents*

Introduction to the Revised Edition

How to Inspect a House has been acclaimed widely for its successful demystification of the house inspection process. However, there have been many changes in the field since the late George Hoffman revised the book in 1979. This edition incorporates those changes.

This updated edition of *How to Inspect a House* is organized to take you through your house as a professional home inspector would. I've included critical information on how to identify hazardous materials such as lead paint and pipes, asbestos, and urea foam insulation. The new discussion on semiannual maintenance (Chapter 15) is a welcome guide for any homeowner interested in conducting seasonal maintenance checks.

Despite the book's title, it is not our intention to do away with professional home inspectors, who play a crucial role in the purchase of a house. Not only will some banks require that your future home be inspected by an expert before they will grant you a mortgage, but you also cannot get homeowner's insurance without such an inspection. But, with professional inspectors charging up to $200 per inspection, it isn't possible to have each house you are considering inspected by an expert. That brings us to the purpose of this book: to enable you to do the preliminary inspections on your own. Your ability to spot flaws and/or strengths in a house will allow you to sift through your selection of homes and save the inspector for the one house that seems most promising.

Steve Horgan

Think Carefully When Shopping for a Home

I HOPE to make clear in layman's language what I think you must know in order to make a physical examination of a house. When used as a guide to diagnose the physical condition of a house, this book can save a buyer thousands of dollars if faults are found, or can give him or her peace of mind to know that the purchase is sound. Homeowners may use this book to look for faults that can be corrected before they become serious.

Although home inspectors are essential in the final purchase of a house, it is not necessary to have every house you look at inspected by a costly professional. When you do decide to hire a home inspector, there are a few things you should keep in mind. Home inspectors are supposed to work *for* the buyer. Remember, the real estate agent is not the home expert. Hire a house inspector who is totally impartial. That means someone who simply inspects the house and submits his or her findings but does nothing whatsoever to correct any fault he or she may find. In that way the inspector will not be motivated to find work. The inspector should be knowledgeable enough to give approximate costs of repairs as a guide so that the client can make a decision on the house. He or she should know, for example, the cost of different kinds of roofing materials as well as the labor costs to install them. He or she should also know what new plumbing and electric wiring costs are.

When you hire a home inspector, beware of "sweetheart" arrangements. An agent may know a friendly contractor or someone with a little experience who will look at your house. The contractor remains friendly as long as he or she makes favorable reports. You must find an independent expert.

When you stand back and look at a house, it looks like a huge, mysterious monster with numerous complexities and hidden secrets. But if you take it apart piece by piece, you can begin to understand it. That is what we are going to do in this book. I am going to take you with me on one of my home inspections to learn, step by step, the physical condition of the structure: that is, drainage, foundation, construction, plumbing, wiring, heating, tile, roof, paint, as well as signs of dry rot, termites, and the like. The tools needed are a steel ball of 1/2- to 3/4-inch diameter, a level, a screwdriver, a flashlight, and a good eye (Fig. 1). With these instruments and some basic knowledge that I hope to impart, you can inspect any house and make your own preliminary evaluation.

The knowledge you gain from this book will be even more valuable if you purchase directly from the seller, who often doesn't know of faults and would be reluctant to disclose them if he or she did. If you alert the seller to these faults, he or she may

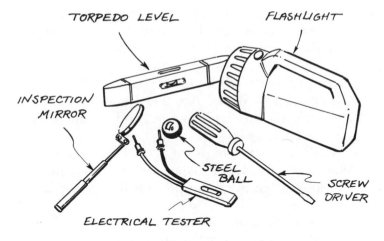

FIGURE 1. INSPECTION TOOLS.

even lower the asking price of the house or repair what is wrong before you purchase it.

First, think about the house and its setting and whether you want to own it. You have investigated the neighborhood for schools, shopping, convenient commuting, sunshine, possibility of expansion, taxes, and the numerous ancillary points of personal taste. Think carefully. Is there a highway nearby? How busy is it? Will it be widened and used heavily, thus creating disturbing noise? Are you pleased with the view? Will it remain as it is? Or is there a good possibility that a development will be going in to spoil your view?

There are many other things to think about; their importance depends on how you think about them. You may want to know the location of the dump and the nature of the trash disposal system in the area. How about of the distance to the airport or fire station and the proximity to movies, bars, or campus life? How about the nature of the neighbors' activities? Is there a swimming pool on the other side of the fence next to your patio? Is your neighbor a weekend mechanic with automobiles parked all about? Are there boats and trailers cluttering the area? Think now, and you might not despair later.

When you get right down to the house itself, consider some important aspects that are frequently overlooked but are as important to a house as its roof.

Take circulation, for instance. A general rule should be to keep traffic out of rooms. Corridors are for passing through to get to rooms. If there is no way to get to a certain room without passing through another room, you have an "obligated room." Sit down and study the circulation pattern. You'll be surprised at yourself once you start giving this important aspect some thought. If you can avoid a mistake later by thinking about it earlier, you're ahead of the game.

I suggest you take time to draw a floor plan; then when you get home, you can study it. Measurements don't have to be precise, but do a little stepping off. Keep in mind that many traffic problems can be changed by moving a door or two. In a large room, a freestanding bookcase or massive furniture can direct traffic in another direction. With your floor plan you can trace in pencil the traffic patterns that members of the family would follow down hallways and through doors. You'll learn as much about that house in an hour as you would in six months of living in it.

We're close to another consideration now: layout. If there's a traffic problem, it may be because the layout of the rooms is poor. Consider your family life-style. Do you use the den for family gatherings, or does your family prefer assembling in the kitchen? If so, can dining be directly off the kitchen? Do you eat from trays while watching TV? Think about it. Would you like the bedrooms and baths to be completely private? Think about acoustic as well as visual privacy.

"Interior zoning" is a good term that describes another important aspect of layout. There are three categories of zoning: work, privacy, and shared activities. Laundering is certainly work and should have its own separate area. The kitchen is another work zone. Do you want to be alone while preparing food, or do you like to talk and visit?

Are you a reader? Can you sit and read in the living room during certain periods of the day without being interrupted by people running through? Do you have a hobby that requires privacy? Keep in mind that there are no absolute rules for the layout of a house. Every family has a different life-style. But think thrice before you buy a house that has to be completely remodeled to get a floor plan that will please you.

Think about safety. Is the house isolated from the neighbors and the street? If so, thieves could break in without being seen. In that case, see that all doors and windows have good locks. Many glass sliding doors can be lifted out of their frames. If locks to prevent this are missing, you could ask that they be installed before the final purchase, or closing. Is there a burglar alarm system? Ask the owner to demonstrate it and explain how it operates. Silent alarm systems to alert police are available, but many communities don't allow direct hookups. Ask. The police urge and invite inquiries about the best kind of alarm system for the area. They know and are eager to help.

A house must have several exterior doors strategically placed in case of fire. You should not have to run through the whole house to find an exit door. A multiple-story house must have approved fire escapes. If you are in doubt about the proper fire escapes, call the fire department. They'll check your house at no cost. Smoke alarms cannot be recommended too highly. The proper location of smoke alarms is important. A fireman can survey a house and tell you the best kind of alarm and where it should be placed.

Please give some thought to the accessibility of your home for handicapped people, taking into consideration the ease of getting about inside the house using a wheelchair or walker. We should all make our homes inviting to persons for whom mobility is a problem.

How to Inspect a House

Foundation and Soil 1

WITHOUT a good foundation, all the inspection we will be doing is useless. We talk about foundations when we think of house support, but beneath the foundation is the footing, which is hidden (see Fig. 2). Its purpose is to distribute weight over a larger area. The footing should be deep enough to reach firm soil and have sufficient steel to give the concrete tensile strength. Cracks in foundations are frequently caused by poor footings or, in some older houses, no footing at all. Old common brick foundations had no footing as a rule, nor was there steel in them. Concrete without steel is worthless for foundations. Without steel, concrete will crack and break apart. Concrete has good compression resistance but little tensile strength. Steel wire mesh is required for concrete slabs, and in some instances steel bars must be embedded in the concrete.

On a hillside, the foundation not only should offer stability on which to build but should also act as a hill-holding barrier. This means it should extend deep enough to be below the zone of moisture change. If it doesn't and the soil is clayey, when the soil is lubricated with moisture, the foundation

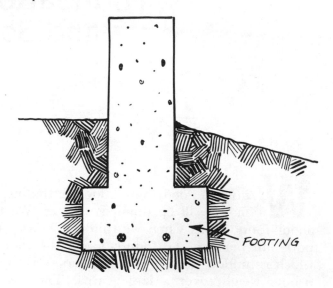

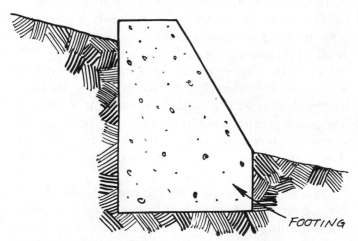

FIGURE 2. FOOTINGS.

could slip downhill, carrying the house with it. We can't determine the depth of the foundation, so we have to look for signs that tell us whether it's deep enough. Hillside houses are more and more common. And in a metropolitan area, or most suburban areas, the best hillside lots have been used, so it's more risky to build on the lots that are left.

Because a foundation is only as good as the earth it's built on, a word about soil is in order. The less you modify the soil, the better your chances of preventing slides. Beware of bulldozers. Removing soil on a hillside to make a shelf is risky, for you have removed the footing of the earth above. Take a small pile of sand and remove a little at the base. What happens? You weaken the footing and the pile crumbles. No support. Geologists would say you have upset the "angle of repose." It's a good phrase, both poetic and descriptive. A hillside that has been standing for many years is in peaceful rest. Upset it and a landslide could occur as gravity works to reestablish the natural angle of repose. If you wonder whether the hillside where the house is located is a potential slide area, walk around and look for large radial cracks that run opposite to the slope. Large cracks could mean an unstable hillside. The soil may be rocky or shaley beneath the surface. It's not firm bedrock. If there's a clay layer, water could lubricate the clay and slippage could occur. Wavelike areas of earth, which show on the surface like little terraced amphitheaters, indicate minor slippage. If you see any, it indicates the soil has slid; how much and how deep is difficult to determine by yourself. If there are trees on the property, look them over, for if the slides were severe, the trees will have a curve in the trunk. This is because trees always strive to grow vertically. Small cracks often indicate rapid drying out of surface soil after a heavy winter rain. They'll close up come next winter. But if the soil situation is suspect, especially on a hillside, I recommend having a soil engineer check the property. He should also consider what effect a new building on nearby property would have.

V Cracks

While inspecting the foundation, check the corners, which are the weak areas. Without sufficient steel in the concrete, the corners could break. Steel helps make the foundation act as one firm unit. Figure 3 shows two cracks in a level perimeter foundation. These are V cracks, wider at the top than the bottom. Undoubtedly the corner of the whole structure has settled. You might find hairline cracks anywhere. I wouldn't worry about them. It's the V cracks that give cause for alarm.

Figure 4 shows a crack all the way through a perimeter foundation. This is a differential settlement due to insufficient steel and/or a footing not down to solid soil.

On a hillside where the foundation is stepped (Fig. 5), A and B are the weak places, for there is less concrete and often insufficient steel. Note the large V crack.

If a house is built on a hillside, chances are a shelf was cut first, earth pushed forward, and the house anchored on the shelf, but much of it built on the downhill side (Fig. 6). If you find this situ-

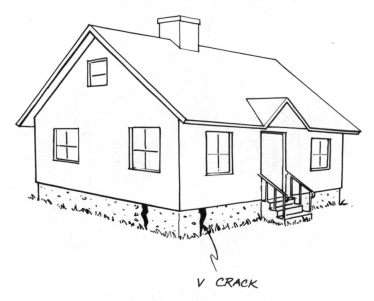

V CRACK

FIGURE 3. V CRACK IN FOUNDATION.

ation, check carefully for weak footing and cracks in the side foundation, for the fill material often settles and slips, leaving the house suspended, on the verge of tipping downhill, or already settled somewhat and waiting for a heavy winter rain to soften the soil some more.

"Oh, that? Why, that crack has been that way from the time I bought the house. Hasn't changed a bit in six years. It doesn't worry me." I've heard remarks like this many times. It doesn't worry him because he's going to sell, or perhaps the man isn't a worrier, period. But neither explanation is assurance that the crack won't enlarge.

It's more difficult to examine the foundation of

FIGURE 4. DIFFERENTIAL SETTLEMENT.

a house built on a concrete slab. You can't get beneath the floor. You can, however, check from the
exterior. Weight distribution is very good initially
with a concrete slab, for obviously the floor is
spread all over the earth and there are no pressure
points. The walls do have weight on the perimeter
because of supporting the roof and perhaps another story, so you might think the slab will crack.
But not necessarily if it's built correctly. The perimeter should have a deep concrete footing with steel.
This footing is a trench maybe a foot wide and
eighteen inches deep (see Fig. 7). Properly built, a
concrete slab has the proper footing, six inches of
crushed rock, a vapor barrier on top of the rock,
then wire mesh embedded in the slab.

FIGURE 5. V-CRACK SETTLEMENT IN STEP FOUNDATION.

Stabilizing cracked foundations is difficult to do properly. One method is to drill holes in the foundation and bolt a heavy piece of steel strapping to it. Another is to bore large holes on a slant, in order to get beneath the foundation, then fill the holes with concrete. In some instances, buttresses are erected. None of these jobs is a weekend do-it-yourself project, except the buttresses, which de-

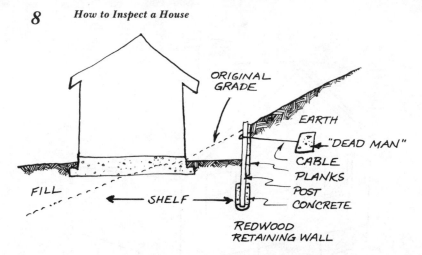

FIGURE 6. HOUSE BUILT PARTLY ON FILL.

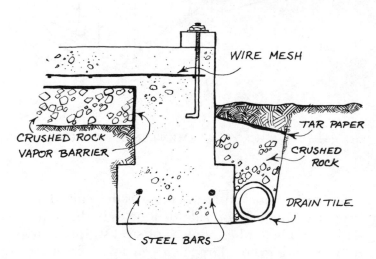

FIGURE 7. SLAB CONSTRUCTION.

mand digging, building forms, inserting steel, and pouring concrete. (A *long* weekend, maybe.)

A foundation that has settled seriously and is threatening the entire house can often be corrected. One method is to dig a hole large enough for a person to work in and deep enough to be about two feet beneath the bottom of the concrete. Using a pneumatic driver, a three-inch steel pipe is driven into the earth beneath the foundation until a pressure of at least 20,000 pounds per square inch is reached. The pipe is cut off and a plate welded on the top. From that plate a jack can be used to put pressure on the underside of the foundation. In many cases the house is lifted to the desired level; then the entire hole is filled with concrete, jack and all. When the concrete dries, the house is secured to the new foundation.

2 Drainage

I F YOU find dampness under the house or evidence of past moisture, it's probably caused by a drainage problem. A wet crawl space, when dried, leaves alligator-hide patterns

Which is more important—good drainage or a good foundation? Both, if possible. What good is a foundation if it rests on poorly drained earth? For this reason I believe good drainage is the most important part of any house. Consider water softening the soil beneath a foundation; the result is mud, softness, and settling. If the house is built on a hillside, a slight slope, lowlands, or a flat area, there are several indicators in the basement (if there is one) that will tell you if drainage is poor.

If all houses could be inspected in the winter, you wouldn't need a chapter on drainage, nor would you have to crawl on your stomach beneath the house to do any investigation; you could shine your flashlight to look for dampness. But, alas, it isn't that easy to do a good job. If the earth shows a little moisture during the winter but it dries during the summer, there's no danger to your foundation. However, if ventilation is poor, fungus can start growing, and you have wood rot. Mold growing on

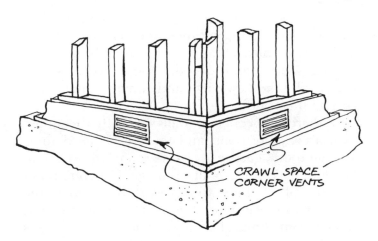

FIGURE 8. CORNER VENTILATION.

the wood is evidence of this. If there is mold, the ventilation may have to be increased. Often there is poor air circulation in a corner, so a screened hole or two can be made in that area (Fig. 8). Proper ventilation prevents mold. How much is proper depends upon the moisture condition—ordinarily about two square feet of opening for every twenty-five lineal feet.

In the summer look for signs of dampness on earth that has dried. If there have been heavy amounts, there will be cracks in the earth. Picture how mud looks when allowed to dry. Often the pattern, as I said, has an alligator-hide appearance. Deep cracks indicate heavy amounts of moisture. When I see this, I look for mold on the wood also. In conditions of poor drainage, the houses that have concrete piers supporting the floor often have unlevel floors. The piers have a small area of weight distribution, and they sink into the softened earth. This causes other stress points bearing additional weight, and soon the house has lost stability. It will take new piers and some jacking up to correct this condition.

If there are concrete walls beneath the house with a concrete floor, and the area is used for a storage room, garage, or game room, you've got to be more observant about drainage. Concrete is not waterproof. If there are boxes stored next to the wall, try to move them, then get your nose in and smell for mustiness; look at the bottom of the boxes for places where water has dried. Look for stained areas on the concrete. When moisture has evaporated, it leaves a yellowish-brown marking. Frequently you see flimsy white fuzz growing on concrete walls. This is a hydrate, called efflorescence, caused by moisture mixing with acids in concrete. It does no harm, but it does indicate moisture behind the wall. If it's slight, I wouldn't worry, but if it's general and heavy, beware of worse conditions, such as a wet basement.

Making concrete walls waterproof is difficult, but there are some good products that claim to do the job. Remember, it's best to prevent the water from striking the wall, but if that can't be done, look into products such as Drylok, Xypex, Thoroseal, RPM, or similar substances.

When you find evidence of much water beneath a house or in a basement, you should first consider whether drain tile can be installed to prevent it. But get prices on the job before you sign final papers, for you may want to change your offering price.

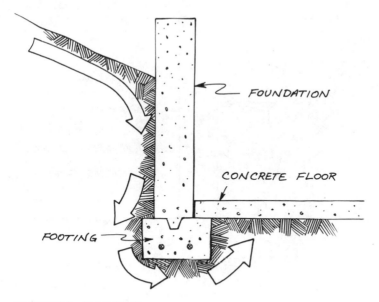

FIGURE 9. TOP SOIL.

Installation

Installing drainage isn't all that difficult. Figures 9 and 10 will help you understand the concept of drainage. The first shows a hillside condition. Much of the rainwater striking the earth above the house sinks into the soil and gravitates downhill. When it reaches the concrete wall, it is momentarily stopped; but as more and more water builds up, hydrostatic pressure increases, and, as stated, concrete is not waterproof, so moisture is pushed through and you have a wet basement. Sometimes you have a concrete foundation that is pushed out of shape by the pressure. The crack between the floor and the wall is a weak place that allows much

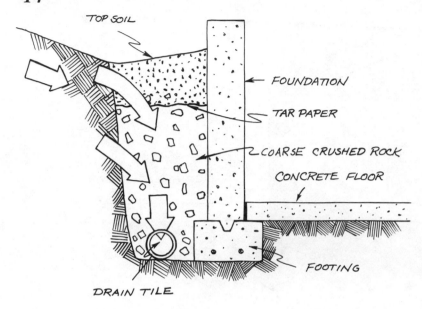

FIGURE 10. DRAIN TILE.

water to pass. If the earth beneath the floor is dense, not allowing water to percolate into it, then more pressures build up and moisture is forced right up through the concrete floor. You've got to relieve that pressure, or not allow it to form. If there's a continuous concrete foundation all around the house, water builds up on the inside of the bottom foundation and makes a lake, sinking into the soil, softening the earth. In addition, this moisture is unpleasant and conducive to fungus.

The ditch is dug on the exterior of the foundation (Fig. 10). As you can see, the deeper the tile, the more protection. A slight slope should be left on the bottom of the ditch. The highest point could be in the middle of the back or uphill wall, with the trench sloping slightly to either direction and carried well past the house and down the sides. Drain tile is laid on the bottom of the trench according to the manufacturer's directions. If plastic perforated pipe is used, remember that the holes should be placed down. Then crushed rock, 1½-inch diameter, covers the tile at least a foot, more if you wish. It's best to coat the wall with hot tar and tar paper before dumping the crushed rock.

The theory is this: as water reaches the crushed rock, it cannot travel horizontally through the rock because of the large spaces between the stones. The water trickles down the stones, reaches the tile, and follows the path of weakest resistance. That is all there is to it. Every situation is different, but the theory is the same.

If there's a concrete patio alongside the back wall, chances are the concrete next to the house will have to be broken up and removed. However, I have seen successful drainage attained by digging the trench eight feet from the house at the edge of the patio. In this case there was a good slope to the concrete which carried surface water away from the house. If there's a three-foot walkway, drainage can be placed outside of that.

You can see that the deeper you lay the tile, the more protection you have. If the wall is eight feet deep, you might get by with going down halfway, but I wouldn't depend on it. The theory tells you why.

If you haven't got time to install proper drain tile before winter, cut interceptor drains in the hillside above the house. These are surface ditches, cut on an angle, that will collect a tremendous amount of water and carry it away before it seeps into the earth. You may be lucky and find they do the job.

Roofs with no gutters spill a great amount of water onto the earth. Sometimes a drainage problem has been solved by adding gutters on the uphill side of the house to collect all the water that would run off the roof and seep into the earth.

Exterior: Paint and Appearance 3

FIRST stand back about twenty feet and eyeball the house from all angles. Line up a wall. You can tell if the house is twisted or leaning a little. Sight down a wall from top to bottom and end to end. The corners should line up. If they are way off, make a note and look for the cause when you get closer. It could be settling in one corner from termites, dry rot, or poor foundations, or maybe it has tipped slightly because it has no diagonal bracing. If the corners are just slightly off, forget it. It could have been built that way. Some are. Or maybe you're looking at a loose corner molding. It happens. Craftsmanship suffers when a contractor wants things done in a hurry. Remember, very few houses are absolutely plumb and level.

Paint

Now step up to the house and look carefully at the exterior paint. There are three basic points to note about paint: (1) peeling and/or blistering, which are nearly always caused by the same fault, (2) checking, (3) chalking or powdering.

PEELING AND BLISTERING: Peeling and blistering occur when moisture is trapped beneath the film of paint. The moisture usually comes through cracks between boards or moldings on the outside of the house, and once in the wall, it wants out. It doesn't all go out the way it came in, so it pushes through the wood and blisters the film of paint. When the blisters get large enough, they split and peeling occurs. Sometimes the moisture is created inside the house. Too much humidity and not enough ventilation is the explanation for that. This is a common fault in snowy areas where winters are long. The house walls are poorly insulated, and too much heat escapes through the walls. As the warm air meets the cold air coming in through the exterior wall, the warm air reaches its dew point, and condensation forms. This occurs on the inside of the exterior skin, or sheathing (Fig. 11). If severe enough, it soaks into the wood, and as we all know, wet wood will not hold paint. If you see peeling and/or blisters of paint, ask when the house was last painted. Paint should stand up four to seven years, depending upon the quality of the paint and the exposure to sunshine. If blisters show on a recently painted house, the cause is undoubtedly moisture forming inside the wall. Later, when you get inside the house, you'll take special care to determine the thickness of the inside wall and whether or not there is insulation in the wall. (More on this later.) I've often heard the excuse, "I got hold of a poor-quality paint and that's what made it blister." It could be true but is not generally so. The seller may honestly believe the blisters are caused by the paint. (He or she doesn't know about condensation within

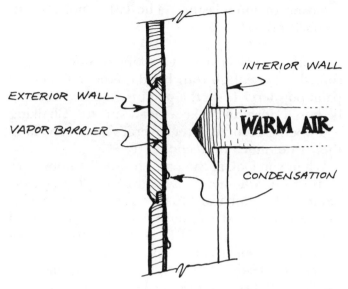

FIGURE 11. DEW POINT.

a wall.) A whole wall of blistering paint is cause for alarm; an occasional blister is not.

CHECKING: Checking, a maze of tiny cracks, is usually caused either by insufficient drying time between coats or poor-quality paint. To correct both checking and blistering, sanding, priming, and repainting are necessary. Sometimes you'll find paint over old checking. A sloppy job, really. It looks like alligator hide. A first-class paint job requires removal of all the old paint down to the wood—a big job. There are various methods, depending upon how extensive the fault: using a hot iron tool made for the purpose, sanding and scraping, using paint remover, or sandblasting. The last is not a do-it-yourself project.

CHALKING OR POWDERING: Chalking or powdering is something else. Rub your hand on the wall. Is your palm powdery? If so, the paint is oil-based and can be hosed down to make a clean surface. Chalking is proper. Of course, after several years of chalking there's not much protection left.

When you look at the paint inside the house, try to find out whether it is lead-based. Lead-based paint is a health hazard that you should pay particular attention to if you have young children. Lead paint tastes sweet, and if taken internally it can cause brain damage or death. Any paint containing 0.5 percent lead by dry weight or 1.2 mg/cm by X-ray fluorescence is considered dangerous.

One way of testing for lead-based paint is to apply sodium sulfide to the paint. If the surface turns black, you know there is lead in the paint. Another type of testing is done with a lead paint test machine. However, this may not be convenient for most home inspectors.

Stained Surfaces

Stain is different. Stain penetrates, paint makes a film on the surface. You can paint over almost all stains, but you can't stain over paint. Stain not only colors wood but lubricates it and keeps it from cracking. Sunshine will dry it out in time. Look closely. If the stain has faded, or if you see several hairline cracks in the wood, the oils have dried out and the stain has lost its power of protection.

Whether they are painted or stained, don't expect all walls to be exactly alike. Sun, wind, and rain act differently on each wall. Sunshine is the enemy of paint, stain, and wood. The more sunshine, the more wear.

Stucco

Is the wall stucco? Most stucco walls have permanent color in the final coat. They don't need paint but will take it if you wish. Scratch the wall and see. The color should be as deep as the scratch. If not, it's been painted. Or find out if the owner knows. Of course, if it's powdered or peeling, you know it's paint.

A few words about stucco. It's an honest product that warns you of the slightest fault. Look carefully at stucco for cracks. Small ones are potential trouble. If moisture gets in, it can swell the wood and push the stucco away from the wall. But worse, a fungus ensues, and dry rot to the wood is the result. Enough dry rot and there's nothing for nails to hold on to and the stucco will fall off.

Where you find cracks that have unlevel edges— that is, one side pulled away from the wall more than the other—you have what is called a differential separation. For some reason there is poor adhesion to the wall sheathing. It may be that the wire beneath the stucco has broken loose. Perhaps dry rot is the cause. But frequently differential separation is caused by a shift in the earth under the foundation, which has caused a board or two to work loose. Look for a settled foundation on one corner.

FIGURE 12. HEADER COURSE IN BRICK WALL.

Brick

If the exterior is brick, you won't know if the walls are solid brick or veneer. But you can quickly learn. A solid brick wall must have bond beams, or a header course every five or six courses. Headers are bricks turned to expose their ends, or running crosswise to the wall (Fig. 12). Look carefully and you can see the headers (narrow bricks). If the wall is veneer bricks, no headers are required. Instead there are metal ties attached to the wooden wall, extending between courses of bricks. If moisture has seeped through the bricks, dry rot could loosen the ties. See that the bricks are flat against the wall.

Windows and Trim

Other exterior surfaces to inspect are windows. The trim may be freshly painted, but check the condition of the wood next to the glass. Frequently putty dries and shrinks, then pulls away from the glass, breaking the seal. Then moisture enters the crack, where it remains without air and starts a fungus, and then dry rot occurs (Fig. 13). Look closely for this. Test the wood with your screwdriver. Is it spongy? soft? If so, dry rot is present.

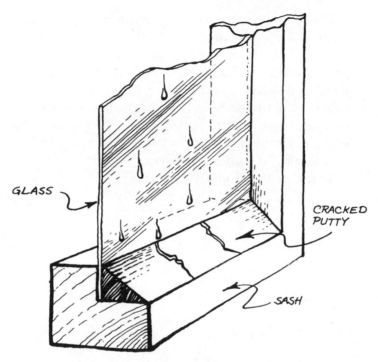

FIGURE 13. WINDOW MOISTURE.

DRY ROT/WOOD ROT: Let me explain something about dry rot. The term is a misnomer. It's plainly wood rot. Wood rot occurs when wood gets wet and cannot dry out with the circulation of air. A fungus starts and feeds on the wood, leaving it weak and useless. You'll find it between boards, especially decks, between stucco and wood, or in wood in the earth, any place where there is a little moisture and no circulation of air. But if you can let air in and stop the moisture, the fungus will die. Any repairs necessary will depend on the extent of the damage.

Those buying or owning a house in areas where winters are cold must check carefully for storm windows. If the house has vacuum-sealed double panes, you're in luck; they offer good insulation. But if you detect a discoloration between the panes, chances are the seal has been broken and much insulation value is lost. Such panes are expensive to replace. Homemade storm windows must provide ventilation, or condensation will result. Look for evidence of dried moisture stains.

Roof 4

I F the seller of a house doesn't brag about the new roof, you can be certain it's old, or suspect. The most common kinds of roofing material are

asphalt shingles
shakes
wood shingles
tar and gravel (also called "built-up" roof)
asphalt and fiberglass (these are recent and very
    good)
roll roofing

There are several other good roofing materials, but they are more unusual. A partial list includes

slate
aluminum
tile
terne
asbestos-cement shingles
concrete shingles
plastic shingles

The attic of a house is a good place to start an examination of the roof. Take a strong flashlight with you and find a way up there (usually through a closet).

There's always dust in an attic. If a leak has occurred, it shows when dried. Look, too, for stains on the wood overhead, especially on the ridge where the rafters meet. Now turn off the flashlight and look around. Do you see shafts of light? Let's say it's a wood shingle roof. If it is, you are likely to see light. If you see it only on an angle, don't get alarmed; but if you see it directly overhead, you should put a piece of paper through the holes. Then when you get on the roof you can see what is causing the holes. If the shingles have worn thin or are completely worn out, you're in trouble, for the sun has probably burned right through the wood. If it's going to take a whole notebook of paper to mark all the holes, forget it. You need a new roof. Yet it is surprising that I frequently find small holes directly overhead and no indication of leaks. We do know that wood swells when wet and this will seal many small holes, but we can't predict such an optimistic cure. We're reporting the condition of the roof. If the holes were caused by sun-worn shingles that have burned right through, chances are that almost all the shingles are thin and won't last long.

If it's a composition asphalt shingle roof and you see holes, remember that no swelling is going to occur to help you.

Shake Roofs

I frequently hear homeowners say that a shake roof lasts forever. Maybe so, but only in cases where the owners have a different idea of eternity than I do. It's true that a shake is a thick, durable-looking piece of wood, but it's still subject to wear. A hand-split, number-one-quality redwood or cedar shake roof with a five-inch pitch will last twenty to twenty-five years in areas where there's strong sunshine six months a year, longer in others. I say hand-split because these shakes will last longer than milled or manufactured shakes. Shakes often get wood rot, but it takes about twenty years. From the ground the shake looks as thick as ever, but "don't go by appearance." If you get on the roof, you may find the wood crumbles beneath your feet. In milling, the fibers are sawn through, disturbing the cell structure of the wood, whereas split shakes break with the grain, and this does not upset the wood fibers. In a hand-split, resawn shake, the split side is exposed to the weather, while the sawn side is smooth and lies flat to the roof.

Wood Shingle Roofs

All shingles are milled, generally from cedar. Shingles have to breathe; that's why you don't find tar paper beneath them, or shouldn't. You can apply composition shingles over wood shingles, but never wood over composition. It's true that the wood shingles beneath the composition can't breathe, but they're no good anyway or you wouldn't be putting a new roof over them.

What you want to look for on a wood shingle roof is how much it has worn. If it has grown thin, it is suspect, for it is brittle and weak and a strong wind will snap it off.

Shingles are not hand-split, and they are thinner

than shakes, so you're right, if you were asking: they will not last as long as their thick sisters, the shakes. But the A no. 1 grade will last seventeen to twenty-two years in sunny areas and longer in climates where summers are shorter. It's not unusual to see shingles worn so thin that only threads of wood are left. "Lacy and leaky," roofers say with glee. But before they become that "pretty," they are thin and brittle. You need a new roof.

Another point to think about is that in some areas—rural ones, for example—the fire insurance rate can be much higher on a house with a wood shingle roof. There are many more fire-resistant materials for roofing than wood.

Is there thick moss on the roof? At the start of the rainy season spread lime on the ridges. The water will wash it down and loosen the moss.

A word about that culprit sunshine. If you could shade your roof, any roof, it would come as close to lasting forever as anything exposed to the air could. It's sunshine that destroys roofs. Look on any roof and you'll find the sides that get less intense sunshine, the east or north, are in better condition than those on the south or west, unless the south and west sides have been reroofed. When a shake or shingle has worn thin or completely through, roofers refer to it as sunburned. It takes several years to wear that much, but it will happen eventually. The length of time depends upon the quality of materials and the intensity of the sunshine. Sapwood (the wood nearer the bark) wears quickly; heart lasts much longer. That ought to tell you to use no. 1 shingles or shakes, for they have no sapwood.

Asphalt Shingle Roofs

The most common roofing material is asphalt shingles. The typical ones come in many grades and colors. They go by weight, which isn't necessarily thickness but rather the quality of material in them. They could be dense and heavy, which is quality without thickness. Roll roofing with a colored mineral surface weighs 90 pounds per 100 square feet. Asphalt shingles weigh anywhere from 200 to 310 pounds per 100 square feet. In the trade this area—100 square feet of roofing material—is called a square. Roofing manufacturers used to have the souls of fishermen—the bigger the better—but they are getting away from the practice of labeling shingles by weight. However, if you ask a few questions, the nominal weight can be learned. A good weight is 265 pounds. Properly applied, a roof of this quality will last fifteen years in the sunny areas of the South and Southwest and longer in the northern states. The exception to the weight advantage is the new asphalt-and-fiberglass shingles. Because of the materials used, they are thin and light but very durable. Their life expectancy is twenty to twenty-five years in hot climates. Remember that sunshine doesn't discriminate: it destroys all roofs and smiles while doing it. When new, composition shingles have a mineral coating embedded in the surface. If most of the surface is black, with only edges of the colored crystals still intact, you can be certain the roof is in poor condition. When the sun has worked on the composition enough to dry it out completely, there's nothing left to hold the crystals, so they fall off. You need a new roof.

Test a shingle carefully by bending the edge slightly. Did it bend or break off? Pinch off a little. If it crumbles between your fingers, you can be sure there's nothing left to turn away water. When it is lifeless and brittle, it has lost all its oils and has become a sponge. It will break off in a strong wind. The edge you broke off should show a real black substance, not grayish black. A good shingle should give with pressure from your fingernail. If it does, it still has life.

Another thing to inspect, without getting on a ladder, is the end of downspouts. If you see a lot of mineral crystals, it's a good sign that the roof is old and worn.

Tar and Gravel Roofs

A tar-and-gravel roof acts in much the same way. The sunshine draws life out of the built-up layers of asphalt paper and tar, and without the asphalt there's nothing left but fibers, which don't turn away water. Look for black spots where the gravel has blown away. If you see a layer or two of split and curled paper, remember it took several years to do that, and several years of sunshine have been working on the entire roof. Beneath that gravel you can be sure the paper has lost much of its life. Also, look around the edges where the metal strip is installed. If the roof is old, it has shrunk and usually is pulled away from the metal. On roofs with a parapet (turned-up edge), the sun wear will be more pronounced on the east and north edge. Check carefully for cracks where the edge turns up. Many tar-and-gravel roofs are flat with a six-inch edge all around. A sprinkler system allows standing water all summer—a good idea since water preserves the roof.

The first and most important point one must learn in evaluating a roof is its age. Ask the owner. If it's a nearly new roof, and you buy the house, ask for the guarantee. The seller won't need it, and you may. At least you'll have the name of the company that did the job.

If it's an asphalt shingle roof, you can see if there are two or more layers of roofing, but you can't tell if a tar-and-gravel roof has been reroofed. If the house is twenty to twenty-five years old, it better have the second roof. A fifteen- to twenty-year-old roof is suspect, especially if it was not a heavy roof. Again, quality pays off. One can buy a three-, four-, or five-layer roof. Each course has hot tar in between, and because the tar and gravel congeal together, ascertaining the life of a tar-and-gravel roof is not an exact science. So much for generalities. Sometimes a roofer will add a new nosing (see Glossary) over the old one. If you find two nosings, you know the roof has been redone. But that doesn't tell you when, so inquire. The city hall may have a building permit record. Reroofing tar-and-gravel roofs is common. All loose gravel is swept off, then more layers of roofing paper and hot tar are added. Good adhesion to the old roof is important. If large bubbles occur, it indicates poor adhesion. The bubbles can split. You should have a roofer look at them.

Slate roofs of poor grade crack and fall off because of the action of freezing and thawing.

Composition shingles and tar-and-gravel roofs can have one of the new synthetic materials added to the surface. Generally this is a pure white substance with white stones embedded in it. This covering will insulate against sunshine to make the house much cooler, but more important, by reflecting the sun's rays it will make the roof last 50 percent longer or more. Thermo Roof is one such trade name. In areas where summers are long and hot, I strongly recommend an application of such a product to the roof.

Gutters

Gutters are necessary to collect roof water and, if possible, spill it away from the house so it won't create a drainage problem beneath the house. But equally important is the fact that without gutters the roof water is blown against the house, wearing away the paint, seeping into cracks in the wall or around windows, and starting wood rot.

Wood gutters can rot and the joints can separate. If they are separated, repair them with a good caulking compound; it will last for years. Metal gutters rust through and have to be replaced. Use your screwdriver and test the gutters in several places. The best wood preservative I know of is Tree-seal. This product is made primarily for sealing large cuts in trees, but when it is used as a wood preservative, there is nothing better for painting the inside of wood gutters. It preserves, waterproofs, and gives life to old wooden gutters.

The best gutters are plastic—no rust, no paint. They are available in almost any color.

In snow country, ice dams may occur along the eaves, and water will enter the walls of the house. The cause is melting snow above the living areas,

which freezes on the colder eave line. One remedy
is to increase the insulation in the attic so that heat
doesn't escape through the ceiling. Another is to
install electric strips of low voltage along the eaves;
this melts the snow and prevents ice dams. These
strips are available in most building supply stores
in snowy areas. You may also see aluminum replacing the lower few courses of shingles. This helps to
prevent ice dams.

Along the eave line is a good place to look for
wood rot. The first sign is swelling of the wood,
often painted over. Press against it with your screwdriver to learn if it is soft.

Costs to repair or replace roofs vary depending
on the quality of the materials used, the ease or difficulty of getting materials to the roof, and the
number of valleys, ridges, vents, skylights, etc.,
which are obstructions and slow down the work. If
you find a poor or suspect roof, get firm costs to
repair or reroof so you'll have exact figures for ne-
gotiating purposes. (More on this in Chapter 14.)
Costs vary for labor and materials in different areas
of the United States, so it is impossible to give
prices here. Furthermore, tar and asphalt shingles
are petroleum products. Their prices change as
often as the wind. What you could do is phone one
or two qualified roofers and ask the average cost
per square (100 square feet) of roof you need.
You'll get a ball park figure, which is something to
go on. Then you be the umpire. Remember: in
summer you think about your roof; in winter you
worry.

$\overline{5}$ Interior

I f the floors are level and the walls are plumb, we won't spend any time underneath the house determining *why* they are. We'll see what the foundation is, but we won't question it unless there is a question.

Doors and Floors

Stand inside the front door. With the door a couple inches from closing, note the distance from the bottom of the door at the knob end to the floor. Now open it wide and note the distance to the floor. Does it scrape the floor? If so, something is out of line. Either the door is not hung properly, the door jamb on the hinge side is not plumb, the hinges are loose, or the floor is unlevel. If the distance is too great, it could be caused by any of these faults except loose hinges. Close the door. Is the crack even on the top and down the lock side? Or does it reveal a wedge of air? It shouldn't. If it does, it probably means the opening is not square. Open the door and put your level overhead first, then on the two vertical sides. These are the jambs. If the hinge side is not plumb, the door will probably stick at the bottom when closed. If it doesn't, it means the door has been planed off. With the door closed, put the level on the hinge jamb. If it leans slightly toward the room, this will cause the door to scrape the floor, or come close. Just the opposite if it leans out. Now use your steel ball. Test the floor all around the doorway. Many times I find the floor unlevel in this area. Unless it's severe, I don't worry too much. That area gets more weather changes than Cape Hatteras. Woodwork shrinks and expands; this can work nails loose. Are the floorboards loose from the joists? Bounce on the floor. Rise on your toes and drop suddenly to your heels. You'll jar your teeth loose but you'll also analyze the floor. If the boards are loose, you'll hear it. They can be renailed. Now step to the middle of the room. Rise on your toes again and come down hard on your heels. Try to see if the floor vibrates and shakes the room and walls. If it does, it means the joists span too much distance without proper support, or perhaps they are too far apart. They are acting like a springboard. You'll have to look at the joists when you're beneath the floor.

Some definitions. Floor joists are the parallel members laid on edge, to which the floorboards are nailed. (When joists are overhead, they are called ceiling joists.) A girder is the heavy piece of lumber on which the floor joists rest. It can be called a beam if you wish, but I prefer "girder." The girders are in between exterior walls and are supported by posts.

If, for example, the floor slopes toward the center of the room, chances are the floor joists are sag-

ging; the span is too long from wall to girder, or
the girder is sagging. Make a note and we'll look
for the cause when we get below.

Steel-Ball Test

A word on the steel ball. This is an important
extension of the eye. It tells you things you can't
see. But it must be remembered that, once it starts
rolling, momentum will carry it far beyond an incline. Stop it frequently, then release it. Use the
steel ball in all rooms. Make notes as to which floors
are unlevel. Having a little diagram of the floor
plan to refer to helps when you're underneath the
floor. Where you have wall-to-wall carpet, the steel
ball is useless. The level and a long board can be
used when floors are carpeted. Frequently floors
slope slightly toward an inner wall, especially if the
wall is bearing the weight of another floor above.
Over the years the weight has caused the joists to
sag, or perhaps supports beneath a girder have
sunk a little. If you can easily get beneath this area,
it is not difficult to add supports to stabilize the
problem. I wouldn't be too eager to jack it up to a
level position. Live with it. Leveling houses can
cause trouble. Windows crack, doors no longer operate smoothly, plumbing can break, plaster and
walls crack. In older houses, the perimeter foundation often settles from years of weight, causing
the floors to sag toward the exterior walls. This is
a major repair job; if the slope is slight, forget it. If
it's extreme, get a contractor's price and opinion
before you buy.

Keep in mind also that green lumber is used to
build houses. When it dries, it shrinks, sometimes

evenly, sometimes not. Once the shrinking has taken place, conditions stabilize. I frequently find unlevel floors but can see no structural fault. However, if you find unlevel floors that slope toward one point—a trend, so to speak—then the cause can probably be explained. Beneath the floor, look for wood rot to posts, a cracked and separated foundation that causes settling, a sagging girder that has posts too far apart, sagging joists that span too great a distance for the weight, or termites that have weakened the lumber. Often, too, a concrete pier will sink into the earth because of softening of the bedding from poor drainage. If you find any of these conditions, the mystery is solved; you can then see what has to be done to make corrections.

Learning what causes faults is fine, but if you can't explain a fault, you've got a mystery. Don't buy mysteries, especially serious ones. Read a who-dunnit instead. Or attend a magician's show. They're the only mysteries you should spend your money on. When the owner of a forty-eight-unit apartment building I examined wouldn't allow me to remove some plaster from a closet wall so I could see what was causing the crack that showed up on all six floors, I advised my client to beware. "Don't pay a half million dollars to buy a mystery." He took my advice.

Plaster Cracks

As you go from room to room, use your flashlight to inspect the walls and dark corners; look for cracks. Plaster cracks are common. Plaster acts the same way as stucco. It's stiff and brittle and will show the slightest movement. There are many causes: earthquakes, green shrinking lumber, poor diagonal bracing, weak construction, and, of course, foundation settling or wood rot and termites. Large cracks should be checked to see if the plaster is pulling away from the wall. Run your finger over it. If one side is raised, it undoubtedly is pulling away. Try to determine the extent of poor adhesion, for this will tell you how much has to be removed and replastered. Bubbles or raised portions are definitely indications of pulling away. Be careful. If you press too hard against them, you're likely to lose plaster. Ceiling bubbles are potential trouble.

One cause of plaster coming away from a wall is moisture. For years there could have been a slight leak that has eventually caused decay of the lime in the plaster; then the plaster literally loses its grip.

Gypsum Board Cracks

Gypsum board cracks are something else. If there are straight cracks, it is usually at a joint. Poor taping is generally the cause. You'll frequently find cracks on either side of a doorway or window at the top of the opening. These are header cracks. Not very important. The header is the large beam stretching across an opening (Fig. 14). Often it is one piece, a four-by-twelve. They're put up green and swollen with water. When they're nailed, moisture splatters from them with each blow. Carpenters like them. "Just like nailing bananas," they say. But you can imagine the shrinkage that occurs over the next year or so. In the meantime, gypsum board has been nailed to the header and the studs, then taped and painted. The shrinkage will not be

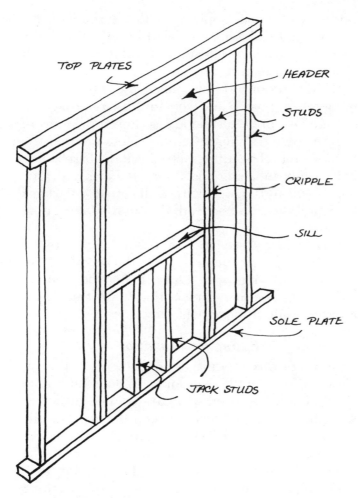

FIGURE 14. HEADER BEAM.

uniform. A crack appears in the gypsum board where the header meets the stud on either side. Once the shrinkage has stopped, fill the cracks with spackling paste and repaint.

If the interior walls are Sheetrock (a trade name for gypsum board) and you find a large diagonal crack, you can be certain it was caused by a severe movement, a shifting or settling. Note whether the floor is unlevel near the wall. Check the baseboard; is it firmly touching the floor? It takes a drastic movement to break sheetrock diagonally. Perhaps we'll find the cause beneath the floor. Make a note to look.

Wherever you see cracks in plaster or Sheetrock, and the edges of the cracks are darkened, it's an indication of moisture—a leak. It may be from an old leak, but be sure. Cracks that have clean edges are the result of movement only.

Testing for Insulation

In two or three rooms, remove the plate from an electric outlet on the exterior walls only. Be sure to check that all exposed wires are connected before wedging the screwdriver between the box and the wall covering (Fig. 15). Do *not* attempt this insulation test if any wires are disconnected. Push the screwdriver gently through to the exterior wall. Feel for a slight resistance; you're determining whether or not there is insulation in the wall. Move the instrument about a little. Nothing? Okay. Try in a few more rooms. One test is not conclusive. You'll know if you meet a spongy resistance; if so, you've got insulation in that wall. It's good to know,

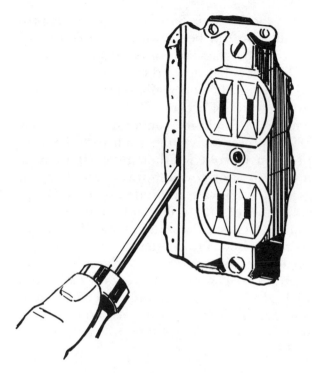

FIGURE 15. TESTING FOR INSULATION.

for it tells you of hidden quality. Later we will inspect the attic for insulation.

A note on insulation. Generally, depending upon
the type of construction, the heat loss and obverse
heat gain in summer through walls is from 15 to 20
percent without insulation. Attics are something
else. If you're going to insulate one place only,
choose the attic. A 20 to 30 percent heat loss and
gain passes through that area. Attics are easy to in-

sulate after the house is built, if the access is provided. Insulation can be blown in in a couple of hours, or the fiberglass rolls or batts can be laid in. Foil should always face toward the living area. The typical do-it-yourself kind is fiberglass, six to nine inches thick, with foil backing.

Remember we spoke of condensation and dew point in the preceding chapter? This can be a serious problem in cold weather areas. If there is enough condensation forming within a wall, it can run down to the sill plate and start wood rot. When this condition exists, the walls, both on the interior and exterior, first show rotting at the floor level. There is not only severe condensation but serious heat loss in the winter. It's a poorly built house. Once the walls are complete, it's very difficult to do a good job of insulating. The only effective way is to remove either the exterior or interior wall. Sometimes it's worth it. More on insulation in Chapter 11.

Diagonal Bracing

I mentioned diagonal bracing; this is very important. There should be diagonal bracing in almost all walls, but you can't detect it if the walls are covered. However, if the house is on a hillside, there's generally space beneath the main floor that is not finished. The substructure posts and beams that are exposed offer an excellent opportunity to look for diagonal bracing in the house. If no diagonal bracing exists, it is a minus, but the braces are easy to apply. When the posts are several feet apart, the diagonal braces should be two-by-sixes, and they

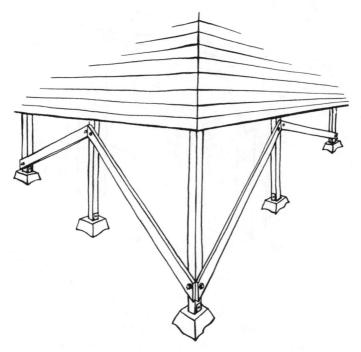

FIGURE 16. DIAGONALS.

should be bolted to the posts, rather than nailed
(Fig. 16).

Another good method of diagonal bracing is the
use of plywood gussets (Fig. 17). Gussets are triangular pieces of plywood ⅝ inch thick or more,
with numerous nails on post and beam. They
should be a minimum of two feet long. The longer
the better. In addition to diagonal strength, gussets
offer excellent fastening where posts meet beams.
Don't trust toe nails; the only good they do is hold
the post to the beam. The use of gussets and/or di-

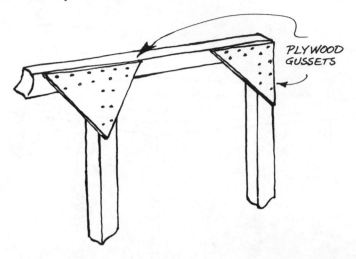

FIGURE 17. USING PLYWOOD GUSSETS FOR DIAGONAL
BRACING.

agonal braces could mean the difference between
saving or losing a house during an earthquake.

A point to remember: sheets of plywood nailed
to exposed studs or posts offer excellent diagonal
bracing and act as a finish material at the same
time.

The Attic

All attics should have ventilation, whether improved or not. If unimproved, they're easy to ignore, but they're not ignoring you. During the
summer a tremendous amount of heat can accumulate in that space, and without ventilation it can't
escape. This is why houses stay warm so long into
the night. Proper ventilation has screened or lou-
vered holes either in the soffits (see Glossary) or
between the rafters where the wall meets the roof,

and up near the ridge line. This allows through ventilation. As hot air escapes through ridge vents, it draws cooler air through the lower vents. In the summer it can lower house temperatures ten to twenty degrees. If there are no vents along the eave line, you can still have them up at the ridge and they will help somewhat. How much ventilation? I've read so many conflicting figures that I'm not going to give any here. I suggest that you check the building codes in your area. But first use your head. If there aren't any vents, there should be. Whatever you add is more than you had.

There are excellent rotor-type ventilators for roofs. They have no motor, but as heat escapes it revolves the finned vent; the more it revolves, the more heat it expels. In some cases a fan is required to do the job.

Note: Attic ventilators should remain open summer and winter. Summer ventilation lowers the attic temperature and cuts down on air-conditioning costs. Winter ventilation removes moisture that could condense in the attic space and start dry rot. In the northern states look for dry rot near the eave line in attics.

Structural Lumber

While in the attic you have an opportunity to inspect structural lumber and methods of building. Look at the size lumber used for rafters and their distance apart. If the lumber used is rough or unsurfaced, it is full-dimensional and stronger than smoothed or surfaced lumber. On a steep roof in snowy states the rafters should be two-by-six, sixteen inches apart, and have knee-wall bracing to

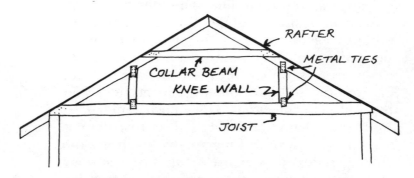

FIGURE 18. ROOF RAFTERS.

support heavy snow loads (Fig. 18). The steeper the roof, the less vertical load the rafters carry. Check also the method of fastenings where knee walls and collar beams meet the rafters. If they are bolted together or have plywood or metal gussets, they are better than nails. That's care and quality. Also, you should stand back from the house and sight the roof. If the ridge is sagging like an old mare's back, beware. Look at the rafters. If they are sagging from the ridge to the eave line, they're too small for the distance they span. They won't straighten up. Bracing can be added to hold them, but it's a poor situation if they dip. Incidentally, a pair of binoculars can be used successfully to examine the condition of a roof, and they are much safer than ladders.

"Can I build a room in this attic?" I'm often asked.

"Yes, but it will require more than laying down floorboards."

Those ceiling joists inviting plywood and carpets are not made to hold much more weight than the ceiling. If you start walking on them, they'll sag. In all probability new joists will have to be "sistered" alongside the existing ones. The new ones will be larger and extend above the old ones, so the weight will bear on them, leaving the old ones holding the ceiling. This is a job that requires experience and know-how, if anyone occupying the attic hopes to stay up there.

In the southern states the roof should have hurricane ties holding the roof securely to the walls. Look for them in the attic. They may be metal strips, angle irons, plywood, or wood.

6 Electric Wiring

T HIS chapter presents the bare necessities that you should know about wiring if you want to examine it. On the other hand, if you choose to take the word of the occupants of the house that because they've had no trouble the wiring must therefore be safe, then skip this chapter. I have attempted to show you the *why* of basic electric wiring and how to check it. Unfortunately for some people, it involves figures, but you'll see they are inescapable.

Electric wiring holds more mystery to the uninitiated than any other aspect of a house. It should. *Respect it.* Yet with a little basic knowledge it is easy to test and examine.

Voltage

To start: if you wonder whether you have 220 volts of electricity to the house or the now uncommon 110 volts, look at the wires leading from the pole to the house. If there are two wires, you have 110 volts, if three, 220 volts. (In almost all cases the voltage is now really 115 and 230.) However, even if there are three wires, you may not have any 230-

volt outlets in the house, but at least you have 230 volts to the house.

A good wiring job has firm connections and splices throughout, but you won't be able to examine all of these because many of them are hidden in walls, attics, closets, and basements. This is the mechanical part of wiring anyway, and although it is important, you mainly want to know:

> Does the wiring meet the code?
> Is it safe?
> Are there enough circuits to serve your needs?
> Are there 230-volt receptacles for the following?
>> stove
>> clothes dryer
>> water heater
>> power tools

Fortunately, you don't have to know all the intricacies of wiring a house to determine if it is properly wired.

Wire Sizes

The first step is to learn the difference between two or three wire sizes. There are only three basic sizes used in a home, and one of those is for special purposes. All wires are measured by numbers—e.g., no. 10, no. 12, no. 14. You should get a short piece of each—four or five inches will do—study them, and get acquainted. If you have Romex wire, separate the black and white, but leave the colored insulation on. Peel off an inch of the insulation on one end to expose the copper. You'll notice that the *smaller* the number, the *larger* the wire. Compare all three; then to simplify matters lay the no. 10 aside, because 98 percent of the wire in a house is no. 12 or no. 14. Take one wire, lay it across your first and second fingers, press it with your thumb. Bend it. Now do the same with the other wire. The no. 14 bends more easily, doesn't it? Now you have two tests: sight and feel. You'll use both when examining, unless you're always lucky and find the number printed on the insulation. We'll go to the service panel in a moment, but first a word about the heavier wire.

No. 10 wire is used for appliances such as stoves, clothes dryers, electric heating, and electric water heaters, and in these cases is 220 volts. In the case of stoves, the code says that if the counter top and oven are not separated, the wire must be no. 6, protected by a 50-amp fuse. This gets too complicated. For now, let's concern ourselves with the ordinary.

Remember this: the larger the wire, the more watts it will carry. So kitchen outlets should have no. 12 wire because the appliances there are used frequently. Any appliance with a heating element uses high wattage. Toasters, for example, will take 1,200 watts or more, waffle irons about the same, hand irons 1,000 or more, and rotisseries perhaps 1,600 to 1,800. Mixers, can openers, radios, and lights take very little by comparison.

Let's start in the kitchen because that's where the coffee is. TURN THE ELECTRICITY OFF AT THE FUSE BOX. Okay, have another sip of coffee and remove the plate covering the outlet staring you in the face. Take out the two small bolts holding the outlet in the box and pull the outlet out a couple of inches. If a good electrician put it in, he left plenty of slack to do this. Can you tell the size of the wire? Try to bend one of them. You're looking for no. 12 wire and hope to see it. If you aren't sure of the size, be sure the power is off, then remove one wire from the outlet and compare the size with your sample. I hope it is no. 12. Check the other outlets in the kitchen. Now go through the rest of the house. You don't have to check them all, but no one is stopping you. In rooms other than the kitchen, most wire will probably be no. 14. This is proper. Living rooms, bedrooms, and rooms where lights, TV, radio, etc., are the principal electric gadgets can have no. 14 wire. If you want to save some time, check the wiring at the same time you check for insulation.

Fuses

All right. Now for some very important figures. Unfortunately you've gotten only half the story. Wire size isn't the only answer. We're now going to check into fuses. At the service panel or fuse box (Fig. 19), with the power turned off, remove the metal plate around the fuses or circuit breakers. Look at all those black and white and red wires. Spaghetti! Don't panic. You won't have to figure them all out. Wires, or circuits, have to be protected by the proper size fuse or breaker. That's where the amps come in. And I know you've heard of 15- or 20-amp fuses. What does it mean? Mathematics may be the answer. Properly, a 15-amp fuse or breaker will burn out or trip when more than 1,725 watts are being used on the circuit it protects, or if there is a short circuit in the line. A 20-amp fuse will take 2,300 watts. But—and this is what you are

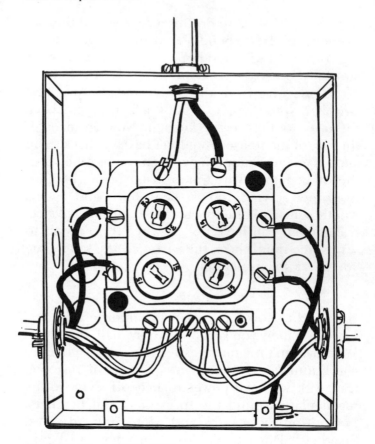

FIGURE 19. A FUSE BOX.

inspecting for—all 15-amp circuits must have no. 14 wire, 20-amp no. 12 wire. Each black wire you see in that panel is connected to a fuse or breaker that constitutes a circuit (Fig. 20). In some cases they could be red. The white wires are ground or neutral wires. Now with your knowledge of wire size, check to determine if no. 14 wire is connected to 15-amp fuses or breakers, no. 12 to 20-amp. If someone has inserted larger fuses than the wire will accommodate safely, you're overfused and not well protected. This means that before the fuse burns out, the wire will overheat and may burn the insulation in a wall and start a fire. Look for labeling of individual circuits. If that has been done, check to see if the kitchen circuit has no. 12 wire with the proper fuse. You can now see why kitchens should have the larger no. 12 wire and a 20-amp fuse, can't you? Multiply amps by volts and you get watts—20 amps by 115 volts equals 2,300 watts.

Take a case where the rotisserie was operating at 1,600 watts and someone decided to iron a skirt for the dinner party and plugged the iron into the same circuit. The iron takes 1,000 watts. Wham! A fuse blows, or should, if it was a 20-amp. But what if someone had slipped in a 30-amp fuse, or used a penny? You know the result: overheated wire and a possible fire.

The use of larger fuses can be prevented. Install nontamperable fuses of the correct amps to correspond to the wire size. They're commonly called Fustats, or S-type fuses.

Many people have told me when I find overfusing, "All I know is I've never had any trouble, so it must be all right." You know the answer: they've

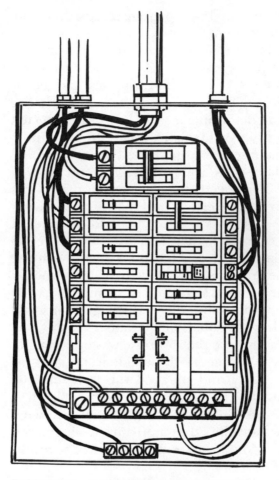

FIGURE 20. A CIRCUIT BREAKER BOX.

been lucky, not entirely honest, or never tried to draw more watts than the wire will accommodate. But new occupants of a home have different demands. So at least start with circuits properly protected.

If you're underfused you're safe. If, for example, you find no. 12 wire and 15-amp fuses, you won't be able to use as many watts on the circuit as the wire provides.

The 30-, 40-, or 50-amp fuses, if properly wired, will have larger wires than we have discussed, no. 10, 8, and 6, to protect large appliances. They'll undoubtedly be 230-volt circuits. I have seldom found appliance circuits improperly wired.

If you find a 20-amp breaker, for example, on no. 14 wire, that's overfusing. The breaker should be changed to 15-amp. The person who installed it may know that the circuit has nothing but lights on it. In that case it's safe, but we can't follow the wire in the wall and don't know.

Circuit Breakers

A word on circuit breakers, as opposed to fuses. Breakers are new and modern and convenient and safe because no one can slip in a larger one, as is frequently done with fuses. But breakers have moving parts, and if they are in an exterior box they can freeze up from moisture and dust; then they won't trip easily. They should be manually tripped twice a year for safety.

Outlets

How many outlets should you have? First of all, remember that an outlet is any resistance, or place where current stops: lights or receptacles. The building code makes it rather clear after the third reading, and not all building inspectors enforce the code in the same way. It says something about having a receptacle every six feet along a wall, excluding openings. It also says there should be one circuit for every 575 square feet. You would be better off if you calculated the square footage, porches included, and divided by 450 to get the number of circuits. You will have some spares if you do that. Actually, I believe that a well-wired house has enough outlets so that a floor lamp placed anywhere along the wall won't require an extension cord. For the kitchen area the code requires two circuits to handle outlets only in the kitchen, pantry, family room, dining room, and breakfast room. Even if you don't have all those rooms, it is wise to have two circuits for outlets in the kitchen.

If you think the house is underwired—that is, has too few circuits—and you want to add more, you'll undoubtedly have to change the service panel. This is the main fuse or circuit breaker box, usually near the meter. You should not consider a box with less than a 100-amp capacity. Large homes should have 200-amp. Local codes in some areas already require 200-amp service. The extra cost is very small. With a large service box you will have a potential of twelve to twenty-four circuits, which is excellent distribution. To learn the capacity of your present box, check the fuse or breaker marked "Main." Its capacity should be marked. If there is no main, a label on the box tells the capacity. In almost all instances, when you add a new box, you will have to provide larger wire from that box to the roof line to meet the service company wire.

Whenever you find a combination of outlets, some of which have the old two parallel slots for two blades of a cord, and the newer ones that have a third U-shaped opening for a third prong of a cord, you should inspect more carefully. The latter kind must have a third, or bare, wire connected to the green screw on the receptacle, as well as to the box, to be properly grounded. What's happening is that do-it-yourselfers are substituting the newer receptacle, forgetting the ground wire because there isn't any. So the receptacle is no safer than the original two-holed affair, and it's forbidden by the code to install them without the ground. One reason that it's against the code is that you are being deceived into thinking it is an individually grounded receptacle. The three-holed receptacles, if properly wired, are safer than the two-holed ones because, should the appliance you are handling become faulty, the current will go through the ground wire before going through you. This is the case if the appliance has three prongs on the end of the cord (male end), because it has the ground wire connected to the frame. The same applies to large appliances, such as washing machines. Don't ignore these safety devices, especially where you are near plumbing, because the water pipes—faucets, too, for that matter—are a good ground and you could easily be touching one.

Testing for Ground Wires

To test if the three-holed receptacle is grounded, the electricity should be left on. Make a tester out

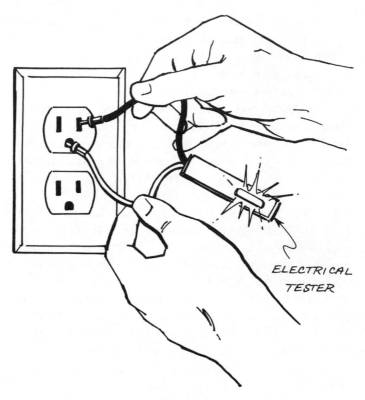

FIGURE 21. TESTING FOR GROUND.

of a pigtail, available in any hardware store, or purchase a small tester made for this purpose. Notice that one of the slots in the receptacle is smaller than the other. The small one is the hot side. Push one end of the tester into the small slot, the other end into the U-shaped hole, the ground (Fig. 21). If the receptacle is properly wired, you should get as much current as you would from the two slots. If you don't get any current, turn off the electricity, remove the plate, and look for the third ground wire. It may not be there. In some areas it is re quired that bathroom switches be grounded.

If you get current from the long slot and the ground hole, you have cross polarity. The hot wire is on the neutral side of the terminals. This is not right and should be checked by an electrician.

Another safety device is a ground fault inter-rupter (GFI). The National Code now calls for new houses to have a GFI for bathrooms and outdoor receptacles. A GFI cuts off the current if there is a leakage to ground of 5 milliamps or more—a good safety discovery.

Aluminum wire is being used in houses because it's cheaper than copper. However, it's not as good and requires a larger diameter to carry the current. If you find aluminum wire, you don't have the quality, but it's not all bad. Strictly speaking, there are receptacles and switches made for aluminum wire. They are marked CO/ALR. The next best practice is to add a short piece of copper wire to the aluminum wire. Then make the connection to the terminals with the copper. In some areas this is not permitted.

The most common use of aluminum wire is for the service entrance and for heavy appliances. If you find this, make certain that the connections at the circuit breaker or fuse box are firm. Aluminum wire has a tendency to back off the screws and un-wind them. Loose connections cause arcing. Arcing is energy, which is heat, which can cause fires. But very little trouble has occurred because of alumi-num wire. Just check the connections once a year.

7 Heating

As I walk from room to room I carefully observe the heat registers. I'm curious to know if the heating system is the gravity kind or forced air. If the registers are overhead, I know the furnace is forced air. If they are on the floor or near the floor, it could be either. If there aren't any registers, the heat comes from another source. There aren't many systems available, and only a few are widely used. Let's look at the most popular ones.

Forced-Air Furnace

Forced-air gas furnaces have a motor that pushes the heat through ducts, which can have long level runs, and sometimes up and down and around obstacles. The unit can be located in the basement, attic, garage, or a closet. They're very adaptable, as you can see, don't take much room, and are very efficient. In addition to pushing hot air through the ducts, the motor sucks cold air from inside the house and reheats it. This cold air is filtered, or should be. I've frequently found filters as dense as a piece of plywood. This starves the furnace of air, cuts down on efficiency, and is the biggest cause of a cracked heat exchanger.

The forced-air oil furnace works in the same way as the gas furnace. The main difference is that the oil furnace has a motor in front of the furnace to pump oil.

Gravity Furnace

A gravity furnace has no filter, no motor. The ducts must slope up from the furnace to the registers so the warm air can rise. A gravity furnace is always in the basement. And the gravity furnace does not have electric wires running to it. There may be small wires, but they are for the thermostat. Since it is without a motor, the gravity furnace is quieter. It is not as quick with the heat, but it has no working parts to break down, and it doesn't blow dust around.

Floor Furnace

A floor furnace is essentially gravity heat, without ducts. The main criticism is that distribution is not good, for you have heat in one place and not in each room. The grill gets very hot, which is a hazard for children, but great to stand over on a cold morning.

Wall Heaters

Wall heaters, sometimes called panel ray, are common. These are space heaters and they do heat the space around them adequately but do not distribute it well. They are good for rooms that may have been added to a house.

Electric Heat

Electric heat is used a great deal. It's good, clean, quiet, and safe if wired properly, with no gases or vents, and installation is generally less expensive than for gas heaters. Intertherm, sometimes called liquid electric, is a perimeter-type heater with a sealed-in liquid that heats grills and convects heat—either 115 volt or 230 volt. Calculate the cubic feet of space in the room; if you figure one watt for each cubic foot of space, you'll be close to the adequate amount of heat using liquid electric.

Hydronic Furnace

Another heating system that is gaining favor is the hydronic furnace. This is forced hot water. Small baseboard radiators are installed and connected to a heating plant and storage tank. Hot water is forced by pump throughout the system. It is very good heat, quiet and clean. In addition, this system can supply hot water instantly to faucets, thus eliminating a hot-water tank. The hot water doesn't come from the boiler but from a coil located inside the boiler, so the water to faucets is hotter than that which goes to the room heaters.

Radiant Heat

Radiant heat is generally from the floor. Pipes are embedded in concrete or sometimes placed between wood floor joists, and hot water is pumped through them. Occasionally you'll find the pipes in the ceiling. Radiant heat requires a large heater to heat the water, a pump to circulate it, and preferably an expansion tank. Various zones of heat control can be arranged when the system is being installed, but not after the pipes are covered. About the only thing you can check for on radiant heat is the pump and whether or not there's a leak in any pipe. Often a pressure gauge is installed in the line, which would tell you if water is leaking. If the leak is large enough, water can be heard entering the pipes near the heater. It is virtually impossible to determine where a leak has occurred in pipes embedded in concrete. If they are copper pipes, as they should be, the chance of a leak is slight.

It's not unusual to find electric radiant heat from the floor or from the ceiling. Both are good.

Checking a Furnace

Forced-air furnaces are the most common because of their adaptability, that is, they can be installed in small areas and, as stated, do not require a basement. Let's look one over.

The most important part of a furnace is the heat exchanger. Essentially this is a metal box enclosed inside the furnace jacket shown in Figure 22. The hot air accumulates outside the combustion chamber and is blown into the plenum. The plenum is the metal box that collects all the hot air. From the plenum the hot air is dispersed through the various heat ducts to different rooms. A serious fault in a gas furnace is a crack in the heat exchanger, because carbon monoxide would leak through the crack and be blown into the heating ducts (follow the arrows in Figure 22).

There are four good tests to determine if the heat exchanger is firm. First, close all dampers but one, as close to the plenum as possible, then turn

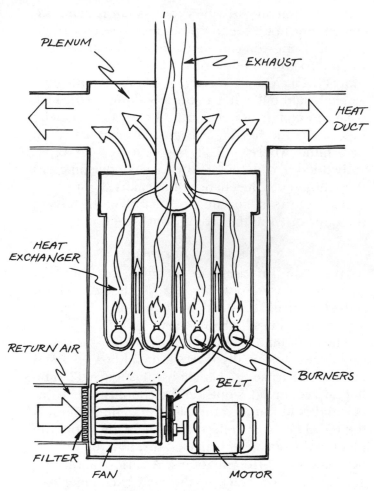

FIGURE 22. FORCED-AIR FURNACE.

on the main flame. Study it carefully to note its color and how it stands up. You can see it through the pilot light hole. Then take your head away from the hole and turn on the blower. If there is a hole in the exchanger, the flame may be pushed out through the viewing hole. The flame should not change. Second, with dampers open, turn on the main flame and again watch it carefully, then turn on the blower. If the flame boils up vigorously or slants off in any direction, it is probably being sucked toward a hole in the exchanger. Again, the flame should not change. These tests take some experience.

Third, use a small mirror on the end of a stick. I have one from an automobile parts store. It is secured by a universal joint. Insert the mirror in the hole above the burners, and with a flashlight you can see an image of the exchanger. Move the mirror around to view as much surface as possible. Frequently you have to unscrew a small plate covering part of the burners to get a better view.

I saved the best test for last. Paint a good amount of oil of wintergreen on the heat exchanger on both sides of each burner. I use a ¼-inch long-handled brush bent at a 30-degree angle. Then, if there is a summer switch, turn it on. Check for odor at each heat register. You should not get any. If you do, beware; you undoubtedly have a cracked heat exchanger or pinholes that are difficult to see. If there is no summer switch, you have to turn on the furnace, then wait for the fan. Don't be in too much of a hurry. Allow the odor to accumulate and seek the holes. The flame will quickly burn away the oil on the exchanger, but the odor will have done the job for you.

If you discover a hole, I recommend that the furnace be replaced. Sometimes the heat exchanger itself can be changed. I wouldn't let anyone weld a hole, and in most states it's against the law. How secure would you feel with a new patch in an old exchanger?

In a gravity furnace it is harder to detect a cracked heat exchanger because there is no blower to suck the air and make the flame boil. If there's a large hole, of course the flame would lean in the direction of the hole. The wintergreen test is very good to use on gravity furnaces. And you should use the mirror to look closely at the heat exchanger. Also, reach in and tap lightly on the metal walls with a small hammer. They should ring, or at least make a hollow sound. If they are cracked badly, you will hear a dead sound. This latter test is not dependable for the novice. Better be sure.

The sure proof of a faulty heat exchanger is actually to see the hole. The boiling flame tests will tell you something is wrong and requires further checking. If you're unsure, you should first ask your utility company to check it. Some do it free. Others have a minimal charge. These companies want good, safe equipment in homes and are very cooperative about such matters. I would always go by their recommendations. They're not in the business of selling furnaces.

A floor furnace is easy to check. Remove the grill from the floor and get down on your knees and look it over carefully with your flashlight. Look for small holes with a little carbon around them. Tap the exchanger; listen. Turn on the flame and look carefully for pinholes in the metal that would show the flame beneath. Also, the flame should burn steadily and not grow or lean to one side.

If you learn that the furnace or heater is in good condition, check the vent pipe to see if all connections are firm, so that it will carry all exhaust gases to the outside. Look at the burners; are they pitted, corroded, deteriorated? If so, you can be sure it's an old unit. Check the heat ducts. Are they insulated? All joints connected? Sometimes dogs get into the basement and run around, knocking against ducts, tearing the insulation loose, dislodging joints. Are there dampers in the ducts? This is important, for everyone has different demands for heat in various rooms, and the proper control is near the furnace. It's not the same to cut off heat at the end of a run, for much heat is then wasted coming all the way from the furnace, and most of it is going to leak out.

Another important aspect of any gas furnace is combustion venting: the presence of oxygen to feed the burning gas. Wherever the unit is placed, there must be oxygen coming into the space. It may be through a pipe from the outside, or, if in the basement, the area should not be closed tight. This is true for gas water heaters also. If the pilot light goes out frequently, it may be from lack of oxygen.

And, of course, the furnace should always respond to the thermostat. Try it and see. In a forced-air furnace, look at the fan housing. If the filter hasn't been changed frequently, this housing can be very dirty. This is dangerous because it will cause overheating. If the fan is belt-driven, handle the belt and see if it is in good condition. They do get old, then split, crack, and break, usually on Christmas Eve. If the unit is dirty and appears untended, it needs servicing, that is, oiling, cleaning, and adjusting. A fire safety technique is checking the area above the heating unit to make sure there aren't any exposed wooden beams. If there are, cover them with a noncombustible material such as metal or a one-hour fire-rated gypsum board.

Older Heating Systems

In some old Victorian homes, especially in the eastern states, it is likely you'll find a steam or gravity hot-water system. In many instances this is a lucky find. These old systems are extremely durable—they're made to last and probably have many years of service in them. There is nothing wrong with them but for two things: (1) from a modern viewpoint they are slow, and (2) many of these older heating systems are insulated with asbestos. Until recently, asbestos was used as an insulator around heating pipes, in heating systems, and in ceiling blocks. When examining an older home's heating system, be sure to look carefully at the heating unit itself. If the unit appears to be covered by a cloth or plasterlike material, you have reason to suspect that the substance is asbestos.

As asbestos is a carcinogen that dries and flakes with age, its presence in house's heating system is especially dangerous. In time, cancer-causing particles are released into the air and are distributed throughout the house with the unit's warm air. The only one who can accurately identify asbestos is a professional. Should you become interested in a home in which you suspect the existence of asbestos, be sure to have a professional home inspector examine the questionable areas before you make a final purchase.

Whatever the case, you'll probably want a new boiler, and it would pay you to get one. The modern ones are efficient and can save you up to 25 percent in fuel consumption. Also, the new boilers are much smaller than the old, put out more heat, and leave more room in the basement. And with a new boiler you can have instantaneous hot water at any faucet without installing a separate water heater.

If you don't like the old radiators, you can replace them with new ones designed to fit along the baseboards. By adding a pump to the system you can have a hydronic heater, as mentioned earlier. This will give you forced hot water. More uniform heat and quicker response will be the result. A few pipes installed at the boiler can do the job. This takes know-how. You should get expert advice.

With forced hot water you can have zone control heating, that is, thermostats installed in several sections of the house to keep some rooms cooler than others.

Judging Heating Capacity

If you wonder whether the furnace is large enough to heat the house adequately, there are many factors to consider. How well is the house built? Is it flimsily constructed, with ¼-inch plywood interior walls and ⅜-inch exterior walls with no insulation? If you have ½-inch gypsum board interior and ¾-inch exterior sheathing, the heat loss will be less. But mainly, insulation and where you live are the biggest factors. There are other things to consider also:

How well or how poorly is the house built?
How well is it insulated?
How much glass is there?
Is the glass double-pane?
Is the house two stories with one furnace?
In what climatic area is the house located?

Even though we live in the United States, heat is still measured by BTUs (British thermal units). The number of BTUs put out by the furnace is important, but there is no set formula for determining how many BTUs will do the job. I've heard of formulas, but I can tell you that in a well-insulated house the number of BTUs required is much lower than heating engineers have demanded in the past. (Incidentally, for practical purposes, one BTU is the amount of heat given off by burning an old-fashioned wood match.)

The BTU capacity of the furnace is plainly marked on a logo plate, usually on the front of the unit. There'll be several figures, but the one you're interested in is the figure after the word "Input."

Another thing to look for is a summer switch. You'll find them only on a forced-air furnace. If there is one, it will be to one side of the front of the furnace and is marked "Summer Switch" or sometimes "Manual" or "Automatic." It starts only the motor. The purpose, of course, is to circulate air through the ducts. It's not air conditioning, but moving air does offer some relief on a hot day. If you like the idea, the switch can be moved to a more convenient location in the living quarters. And if there isn't a switch, it can be installed.

A word of caution. There are electric wires leading to the furnace, and there should be a switch in the line. It may be on the outside of the furnace or on a wall nearby. It's almost always a regular wall switch, like the ones you have for lights, and serves to cut the electricity while servicing the furnace. It is not the summer switch.

Wood-Burning Stoves

In conclusion, I want to say a word about wood-burning stoves. Don't put them down. Wood stoves offer an alternative method of heating homes in areas where wood is abundant. For your safety, the walls adjacent to the stove as well as the stove's foundation should be made of noncombustible material. Examples of noncombustible materials are millboard, brick, and concrete. The stove should be eighteen inches from the wall.

Install one; you'll have a new friend if you do. It's great heat. Check around; there are many excellent stoves on the market. Consult *The Mother Earth News*. It can give you much information on wood-burning stoves.

A note on these stoves: use seasoned wood only (aged about a year). Burning freshly cut wood creates a chemical called creosote, which is bad for your lungs and builds up rapidly in the flue.

8 Plumbing

I F you keep your wits about you, you'll see strange things while walking around inspecting. In a two-story house, ask where upstairs bathrooms are located. Then look carefully at the ceilings beneath the bathrooms. You might see a stain or, worse, a spot where the paint is peeling. If this is the case, you can be almost certain of a bathroom leak. Don't let the seller tell you it's the result of a champagne explosion and he left it there for sentimental reasons.

Bathroom Leaks

There are two common causes for bathroom leaks. One: the toilet seal has broken; repairing this is not a major job. Two: careless showers. Water gets between the curtain and tub, runs down the side, and settles at the floor. When there's enough, it seeps through. If there's a glass sliding door on the tub, turn the shower on. Direct the stream against the door. Close the door and watch for water seeping out between tub rim and door seal. So you got a little wet. Sorry. If there are leaks, the door frame will have to be resealed. Another cause of leaks is the breaking of the seal between the faucets or tub spigot and the wall. There could be a hairline crack. You have to deflect water against the wall to detect this leak. Then get under the floor and look for water or water stains.

If there's a stall shower, a good test for a leak is to lay some paper over the drain and fill the shower pan with two or three inches of water. Let it stand for fifteen minutes or more, then go below to look for leaks. You're mainly testing the pan itself, where it meets the walls, and where the pan meets the drainpipe. In some states, this is a standard test used by termite inspectors. Afterward, let the water drain and check the drainpipes for leaks. Look carefully also around the shower opening. If the curtain has not done a good job, there could be leaks in that area.

One test for a broken toilet seal is to flush the toilet, then lean down and, using your flashlight, inspect the floor around the bowl. Try to move the toilet. Straddle it, grip the bowl with both hands, and try to tip it from side to side. It shouldn't move. If it tips slightly to one side, the seal could be broken. Check to see if the wood adjacent to the toilet is wet or swollen. You may not want to do it, but I rub my finger along the angle between the bowl and the floor, looking for moisture. These tests are not conclusive, since the leak has to be severe for moisture to show up at floor level. But if the seal is broken, moisture will collect between the floor and the bowl. Dry rot will result.

If the moisture on the ceiling was not caused by any of the points just covered, it undoubtedly comes from a source pipe or drain, from either the tub or washbowl. This could be expensive to repair, for a portion of the floor will have to be removed. Think! If you still like the house, make an offer on condition that the leak is repaired. If it's your own house, repair it.

Water Pressure

While you're in the bathroom, turn on the tub water, leave it on, turn on both faucets of the washbowl, but keep an eye on the tub flow. Note how much it diminished in force. Flush the toilet. Is there much loss of flow in the tub and washbowl when water starts filling the toilet tank? If the shower is separate, test that at the same time. Are you getting enough water for a shower, or just a trickle of irritation? If you've got two bathrooms in the house and more than one urgency, you can imagine what will happen in the morning when you're trying to shower. The same thing will happen to the shower when the kitchen faucet is turned on. If the flow is unsatisfactory, you can be certain the plumbing is galvanized steel.

Over the years, mineral deposits and rust have accumulated inside the pipes until there may be only a small opening left. This, of course, increasingly restricts the volume of water. If the pipes are made of lead, their disintegration may result in your ingestion of particles that cause lead poisoning. All water pipes should be made of copper. If the seller does not know what the pipes are made of, have a professional plumber examine them before you make a final purchase.

But, before you replumb, ask the water company to check the pressure at the main in front of your house and again at the point where the pipe enters your house. If there is a big difference in pressure, the pipe from the main to the house should be changed. Often these are very old pipes and a great deal of mineral deposit has built up inside them. It has happened that a house has been replumbed with no appreciable increase in pressure, simply because the pipe from the main to the house was poor.

Pipes and Joints

Sometimes miracles happen, but don't depend on them. Those little valves you see beneath the washbowl, toilet, and tub are called angle stop valves. They are natural traps (Fig. 23). Replacing them often helps the problem 50 percent. Other culprits for collecting rust particles are elbows, mainly the ones that turn from horizontal to vertical. Rust drops down the vertical and rests in the ell, builds up, and constricts the flow. These elbows are quite easily replaced. All these measures aid the force of flow. Of course the ultimate answer is to install copper pipes. Copper pipes are a superior product and do not create rust buildup.

I forgot one other point about galvanized pipes. The horizontal pipes collect mineral deposits more than the vertical pipes. Often, replacing the horizontal ones will provide all the water you need. If not, you can still replace the verticals.

After you've run water, check the P traps for leaks. Run your hand over them. Observe. P traps are the curved drains, usually chrome, beneath sinks and lavatories (Fig. 23). Check the angle stop valves for leaks. Remember to flush every toilet in the house and turn on every faucet. This will test

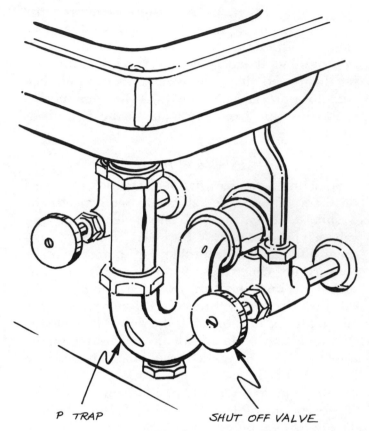

P TRAP   SHUT OFF VALVE

FIGURE 23. P TRAP AND ANGLE STOP VALVES.

not only for force of flow and volume but also for leaks in the drainpipes and the toilet seal.

Faucets and Flows

Another thing I do is to time how long it takes for hot water to arrive at the kitchen faucet. If it takes much longer than ten seconds, it's probably because the water heater is a long distance away. "So what?" you may ask. "A waste of energy," I reply. The kitchen faucet is the most used item in any home. A ½-inch pipe twenty-five feet long contains more than two quarts of water. The water standing in that pipe has been heated once and allowed to cool. When you turn on the hot water faucet, that water is pushed out and wasted, then replaced by another half gallon which has been heated and left standing in the tank. This happens several times a day. Multiply that by the millions of homes with similar conditions, and you realize the vast amount of wasted energy and water. It would pay to move the tank closer to the center of the house or to insulate the pipes.

While turning on the faucets, did you notice that some of them leak from around the handle? Write it down. They should be repaired. Often this is the cause of moisture beneath the sinks or basins, for water gets between the faucet and the surface and drips. The cause of this is poor bonnet packing (see Glossary). Thousands of articles have been written on how to change washers to stop drippy faucets, but few mention bonnet packing. Changing washers won't prevent leaking bonnets. If you're going to do the job yourself, here is one simple remedy. Remove the old packing and wrap the stem with ordinary cotton string to fill the void of the bonnet. With this method there's no need to have a certain size of bonnet gasket. String can be wrapped to fit any size. It will last five years or more. I've never known a plumber who didn't carry a ball of cotton string. With that he can meet most emergencies. He uses string many times in place of gaskets in the large chrome nuts on the drainpipes beneath sinks. You can too.

Sometime after testing all plumbing fixtures you're going to have to get beneath the house and crawl on your knees and walk on your elbows. In tight places you may have to lie on your back to look up at the underside of the bathroom. Curse if it helps. Take a screwdriver, flashlight, and patience with you. Look carefully for leaks beneath toilets, tubs, sinks, showers. If any wood is moist or stained, prod and poke with your screwdriver to detect if there is wood rot. If you found no leaks, you gained assurance. But if there are leaks, make a note that you want them repaired before you buy the house. If there is wood rot, check to learn whether a portion of the floor will have to be replaced.

How do you know where the toilet sets? Easy. Toilets have to set directly above one of the large pipes you see disappear through the floor. Almost always it is a four-inch pipe, usually cast-iron but in old houses it may be lead, in new houses, plastic. There may be two such pipes close together, but one of them is the vent pipe. If you can't determine which is which, look carefully for leaks around both of them.

Don't hesitate to buy a house because the toilet

seal is broken and you have visions of unreasonable plumbing bills. A plumber can reset a toilet with a new seal in forty-five minutes. Or you can do it yourself in twice the time.

While under the floor, calculate the ease or difficulty for yourself or a plumber to get to the pipes if trouble should occur and you need help (usually on Thanksgiving). This factor has a decided influence on the value of the house. Look for clean-out plugs in the drains. Clean-outs are plugs with square heads to receive a wrench, often at the ends of lines. Sometimes they are on a Y on verticals, or horizontals. If you see several of them, there's a built-in convenience (Fig. 24).

Water Heaters

Were the fresh water pipes insulated? This is essential for houses in the Midwest, East, and North. Check the insulation. Add more if necessary. This is a case where too much does no harm, except to purse and back if you are doing it yourself.

There must be a water heater somewhere. Determining its age is difficult. Look for a tag with the date of installation. Can't find one? Not surprising, unless it's only two years old or so. Age and capacity are important, as well as quality. Glass-lined water heaters are the most common. You can expect ten to fifteen years' service from them. Monel- and copper-lined tanks will last longer. Tanks are always labeled, so you will know which kind you have.

Start your examination by asking the owner if he or she knows the age of the heater. Time passes quickly, so add two or three years to the answer,

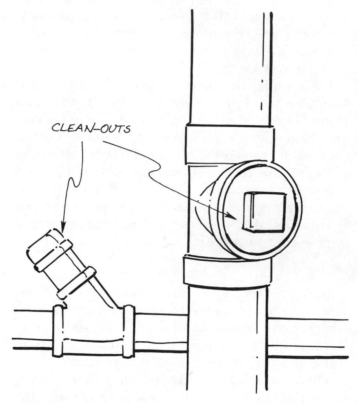

FIGURE 24. CLEAN-OUTS.

unless you are shown the dated installation bill. Look carefully for moisture beneath. If there is some, be certain it isn't a drip from the drain valve, which is near the bottom. Put your hand on the end of the valve. No moisture? Then the tank is probably leaking. They don't cure themselves. The tank itself is inside the thin metal casing, plus an inch or so of insulation. There's no telling where the hole could be, and patching is out. If it's a gas- or oil-fired heater and the burners are pitted and corroded, it's an indication of age or of frequent heavy use. Its life expectancy has been shortened. Check the temperature setting. If it's at the hottest level, it could mean the tank has a difficult time providing water for the household. How many people are living there? What size is the tank? A thirty-gallon tank should be adequate for three people, a forty-gallon for four. I'm referring to gas- or oil-fired tanks. They have a high recovery rate, oil better than gas. Electrically heated tanks can't match them, so larger tanks are required.

Look at the pipe connections at the top of the tank. If heavy rust shows, it was caused by a leak. Maybe it has stopped leaking. Dig a little away, but be aware that you may start the leak again. It could be a rust-through spot, brought on by electrolysis. If copper pipes are attached to steel pipes an inch or so above the tank, there should be either an insulated union connecting the two or a short piece of brass pipe between copper and steel. In the trade the union is called "dielectric," and the point is to prevent electrolysis. There should also be a valve on the cold water side near the top of the tank so you can cut off the water in an emergency. And there should be a safety relief valve on the hot water pipes or on the tank itself (Fig. 25). A pipe should lead from the valve to drain hot water to a safe place, usually through the floor into the crawl space.

GAS- OR OIL-FIRED TANKS: A gas- or oil-fired tank will have a vent pipe. Check the pipe for firm con-

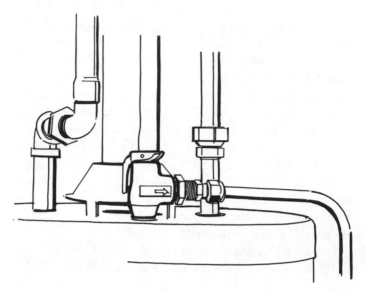

FIGURE 25. SAFETY RELIEF VALVE.

nections and rust. There must also be combustion venting—fresh air leading to the area. If the tank is in an enclosed area there should be a three-by-six-inch hole cut into the door top and bottom, or a hole in the wall to the outside. Sometimes there's a hole in the floor to the crawl space, or air is brought in from the roof. Fresh air allows the flame to burn hotter with more efficiency. Check the gas or oil lines for leaks. Use a small paintbrush and apply detergent mixed with a little water to each fitting. Bubbles will appear with the slightest leak. Poor oil fittings will drip oil.

ELECTRIC WATER HEATERS: Electric water heaters require 220 volts of electricity and must have their own circuit. The size of the wire and circuit breaker depends upon the wattage. The average heater has two elements that heat alternately, usually 4,500 watts. Be sure the wire is the right size to accommodate the amperage of the breaker.

Gas- and oil-fired water heaters should be drained occasionally to get rid of the deposits that settle at the bottom of the tank. Too much deposit acts as insulation through which the heat has to pass to reach the water. The proper draining procedure is to cut off the water leading into the tank, then turn on one or two hot-water taps upstairs, attach a hose to the drain valve at the bottom of the tank, and open that valve. Allow the water to run through the hose until clear. If that's too much trouble, attach a hose to the drain and open the valve. That method stirs up the water more, but it's better than no draining at all. Incidentally, if you hear rattling and banging in your plumbing system, the cause is often deposits in the tank. A good draining is called for, or look into deliming.

9 Fireplace

DON'T overlook the fireplace. Carefully check all the bricks and mortar joints on the facing. The weakest point is below the mantel and above the lintel.

Lintels and Mantels

The lintel is a heavy piece of metal that supports the bricks over the opening (Fig. 26). It's not surprising to find a mortar crack running in a zigzag pattern from the lintel to the mantel. Hairline cracks are common. But if there's a wide crack, say ⅛ inch at the lintel, growing thinner as it rises, it could mean that the lintel is weak from rust and age and starting to sag. You know it won't get any stronger. Hold a straight edge up under the lintel to determine the severity of the sag. Lie on your back on the hearth and look up. Inspect the lintel. Replacing this is a major job.

Another thing to look for is whether any of the facing bricks are coming loose from the wall. Check to learn if the mantel is level. If it isn't, it could mean the whole fireplace unit has poor footing and is settling into the earth. If this is the case, the fireplace is independent of the floor, and you can

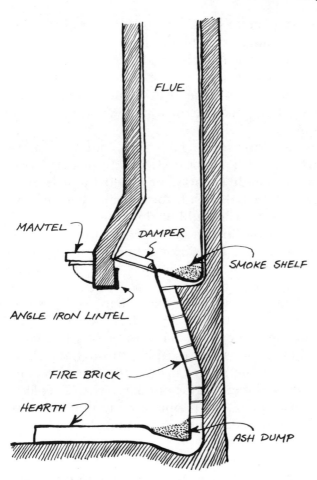

FIGURE 26. THE FIREPLACE.

notice the line of bricks at floor level and whether they maintain a straight and level line.

Sometimes the hearth is laid directly on the floor. If this is the case, notice if the floor is sagging, causing a crack where the hearth meets the vertical bricks. Then check below for the condition of the supports.

In many areas it's against the code to rest the hearth on the floor joists. If you find such a condition, I wouldn't worry, provided there is extra support directly beneath the hearth. The support may be posts, or it could be double-up joists.

Use your flashlight to look inside, up the flue. Is there a damper? Does it operate? Try it. If there's no damper, it's a minus. It has been determined that in an average-size fireplace the heat loss without a damper, or with one wide open, is 14 percent. And not only that, but a slight draft of cold air persists in the wintertime, scuttling across the floor, drawn by the warm air escaping through the chimney. (This is the main cause of the common complaint of cold feet.) In the old days, when fireplaces didn't have dampers, people used to put a piece of cardboard in the fireplace opening.

Dampers

In the summer, insects enter the house through an open damper. With your screwdriver, jab at the firebricks. Note if they are loose. Test the grout between the bricks. In time it deteriorates. (That's getting to be an overworked word. Sorry.) If enough grout falls out, the bricks will follow. After all, it's what holds them in. It's not catastrophic if you find loose bricks or missing grout. Nine times out of ten you can make the fireplace as good as new with an hour's work. Scrape out old grout with a screwdriver. Get a little vicious; this is not brain surgery. Clean it deep. From a building supply store buy some fireclay; the kind mixed with sand is best. Mix with water to a heavy paste or mud. With a broad knife or putty knife, force the mud into the cracks. If you're not good with the knife, use your fingers. But force the mud all the way in. Mud on top of mud. Let it dry for forty-eight hours before a fire is lighted. The slower and longer the curing period, the less chance of cracking.

Sometimes I find bricks crumbly, cracked, chipped, loose, and falling out. These should be replaced. A mason should do this job. Get a price. All these figures will tell you what to offer for the house. At the same time, ask about installing a damper, if the fireplace doesn't have one. The gravity kind can be installed in a ready-built fireplace.

Bricks and Grout

There's something good in everything, and the more you can see, the better for you. Those burned-out bricks and loose grout tell you that it's a good fireplace, for it has been much used, and who's going to use a smoky unit? I'm suspicious of a clean, unused unit. Igniting a piece of paper to learn if it draws well isn't conclusive evidence that you're going to be able to sit around a fire and enjoy a long evening with brandy and backgammon. It may smoke enough to cure a ham. I can't tell you how to determine whether a fireplace smokes each time it is used. Some of them are temperamental.

But there are indications that will tell you if it is an inveterate smoker. Start by asking the owner. Honest people do exist. Look for carbon or black stains on the face above the lintel. Have stains been recently washed off? Has a metal shelf, canopy, or hoodlike affair been added? If so, it is there for one purpose only; the fireplace was a smoker and may still be. Often the hood cures the problem. But there are other ways to correct the fault if you don't like the looks of the hood. First make sure the chimney is not stopped up or practically choked by fallen bricks, which is rather common. Note if surrounding trees or tall structures cause eddies down the flue. This frequently happens. The fireplace may predate a new building nearby or the trees may have grown since the house (and fireplace) was built.

If none of these things are visible, you should next determine if the fireplace has the proper proportion between the size of the opening and the cubic area of the stack or flue. If you don't mind cluttering your head with figures, here is the rule of thumb for the proper proportion: the flue area is equal to $\frac{1}{12}$ the fireplace opening, if the flue is more than twenty-two feet high. If less than twenty-two feet, the flue area should be $\frac{1}{10}$ the opening. You can't do anything about the area of the flue once it's built, but you can increase the height to provide more draw. For a test, get a piece of sheet metal, wrap it around the top of the chimney, first removing the cap; hold it with wire, adding two or three feet to the height. If this cures the fault, erect something permanent. Another test is to cut down on the size of the opening. Build a fire and hold a piece of wood or metal across the opening at the top. Lower it until the fire stops smoking. Mark the lowest edge. This tells you how low the permanent opening should be if you choose to do this rather than adding to the chimney height. A mason could bridge the opening with bricks if you like. Or have a hood built and installed. Good luck. Enjoy the brandy.

10 Tile

T HAT nice tile job you saw in the bathroom looked new, shiny, entirely waterproof, and durable. But is it? If your family takes many showers, you want a high-quality tile job. The tile itself may be of good quality, but what method of application was used? That's the test. If it was a handyman's job to prepare the house for selling, beware; he undoubtedly used mastic and glued the tile to the wall. Even that could be all right, provided the wallboard was waterproof gypsum board or exterior plywood, or if a special waterproofing agent had been applied to a nonwaterproof wallboard before the mastic was used.

Tile Application or the "Mud Method"

The superior method of tile application is the use of mortar. Mud, it's called in the trade. The mud method is definitely not do-it-yourself. You should know the difference between mastic and mud so that you can determine what you're buying.

Using the mud method, a layer of asphalt felt is stapled to the wall, then stucco wire, then floating screeds a half-inch thick are attached. Next, mortar is applied and smoothed to the thickness of the

90

screed boards. When this is properly cured, the tiles are applied, using a beating board to knock and press them into position, forcing them firmly into the mud on the walls. After suitable drying time, the grout is added to fill the cracks between the tiles. Sounds easy, doesn't it? It is, after about the fiftieth time.

Okay, so why is the mud method superior to the mastic? Because hairline cracks frequently occur in the grout between tiles. Cracks so small you can't see them. Moisture gets in the cracks. If the tiles are glued on with mastic, the moisture could soften and swell the backing, thereby pushing the tiles off the wall. If hairline cracks occur in a mud job, the moisture would have ½ inch of concrete to get through before it reached the wall, which has tar-paper protection. That's quality. No worries, unless you don't like the color of the tiles. Sorry; they're there to stay. However, there are extra-thin tiles on the market, made primarily to be installed over existing tile walls. All that is required is that the existing tile be securely attached to the wall. Loose or nonceramic tile will not afford a proper base. These thin tiles come in two different forms, depending on the method of application. One has glue on the back with a protective paper. Simply strip off the paper and place the tile in position. The other is used with a special mastic that is applied to the wall before the tile is applied. In either case, grouting is done after all tiles are in position. So if you find purple, pink, or puce tile, you *can* do something about it.

I run the handle of my screwdriver over the tiles on a wall. As it bounces along, I listen carefully for hollow sounds which would indicate loose tiles. A little tapping is good, also.

Mastic versus Mortar

How can you tell which method of application was used? You've probably figured it out already. With mastic, the tile is directly against the wall, and you can see this along the edge. The edge is curved (nosing tile), but the finished surface of the tile is ¼ inch from the wall, maybe less. With mortar the tiles stand out more than ½ inch from the wall. Special round nosing tiles cover the borders, and these tiles touch the wall, but they're thick enough to cover the half-inch of mortar.

If you find aluminum or plastic tiles, you've found trouble, generally. Many times these tiles are painted, so it's a little difficult to tell what they're made of. However, aluminum or plastic tile is thinner than ceramic tile. Look at the edge and you can tell the difference. When I have doubts, I use the sharp point of my knife and test. Plastic and aluminum are soft. The reason they spell trouble is that no grout is used to seal between the tiles. Moisture can easily get between the cracks and soften the backing. Many people learned this too late, and that's why they painted them. They hoped to seal the cracks with the paint. Don't depend on it.

Counter tops, especially in kitchens where standing water more easily seeps between tiles, are more vulnerable to damage if tiles are applied with mastic. Remember to jot down these points in your pro-and-con columns.

Quality 11

HOUSE inspection is essentially looking for faults, but it is not all negative. While poking and prodding about, you may find hidden quality also. If you're buying, it's good to know where your money is going.

Hidden Quality

In the last chapter we mentioned the difference in quality between a mud and mastic tile job. There are several other important differences between a carefully built house and a zip-zap piece of construction, which I believe are worth mentioning. Why? Because many people believe that the new and better fixtures and appliances are reserved for the rich and will not fit in an old house. That's wrong. Anything that's in an expensive house is available to all of us if we will only spend a little more money, which buys us economy in the long run. Quality adds up to more comfort and less trouble. Take faucets, for example. The best-quality faucet operates freely, consistently, and positively and seldom drips or spills water from around the handles. They're a pleasure to use. No cursing or frequent disassembling. There are toilets that flush silently and refill without a sound—entirely unlike the cataract of roaring water in a cheap one. There are furnaces that cannot be heard, yet the house is a uniform temperature all the time. Electronic filters or air cleaners can be added to any forced-air furnace. They draw and collect tiny dust particles which go right through ordinary filters into the furnace and are baked and blown right back into the house for you to breathe in and sneeze out. Another good product is a day-and-night thermostat, which automatically reduces heat during the night and increases it early in the morning. There are garbage disposals that emit a low hum no louder than the water running into the sink. There are doors that are heavy and close with a satisfactory finality, light switches that are silent and don't interfere with the radio.

Bathtubs can make a big difference. A steel tub is thin, and so is its porcelain surface, so the porcelain cracks and flakes off more easily. Not so with a cast-iron tub. The latter will hold thicker porcelain for a much longer life. To tell the difference in tubs, rap the side with your knuckles. The steel tub is thin and rings, whereas the cast iron is thick and makes no sound, like a rock.

The best toilet made will fit in a forty-year-old house, as will the best faucets. Furnaces can be made quieter by the use of insulating couplings or flexible fiber tubing on the cold air return, or heat ducts. Solid doors will fit any opening. Locks fit any door. A good garbage disposal is heavily insulated and made with better gears and longer-lasting cutters. It does more work faster and is more durable.

The majority of the items mentioned above are the most-used items in any home. It pays to have them of good quality.

If you are remodeling extensively, think about these points. Give yourself a treat and live like the rich in your own old house. Remember, when you spend money for something you could have gotten more cheaply, it only hurts for a little while. After the pain is over, you'll be glad you suffered it.

Insulation

There is much talk about saving energy, and rightly so. We have to do better, and there's much we can do. All houses are someday going to need new appliances. When that time comes, and you live in an area where natural gas is the fuel, please consider getting pilotless appliances. At this writing nine states now require pilotless furnaces (electronic ignition) on all new residential buildings. More states will follow. But before that time comes, look into retrofitting your present appliances. When you consider the number of pilot lights that are burning in your home twenty-four hours a day, you get an idea of the amount of gas wasted each year in the United States. This waste could all be stopped with pilotless appliances, and should have been a long time ago. In the meantime, matches still work.

Insulating a house properly will save more energy than any other program. But how much insulation is proper? Each climatic area makes different energy demands on a house. The building codes should be checked for recommendations. Asking an insulating company how much insulation you should have is like asking a Toyota dealer what make of car is good to buy. There are basic facts one should know about insulation. Once they are understood, you can make a wise choice and not be fooled by anyone.

R-VALUE: Insulation is measured in R-value, which simply means the ability to resist the passage of heat. All products have insulating value; some more than others. Anything dense, such as wood or concrete, is poor. Trapped air bubbles are good. The higher the R-value, the better the insulation. When buying insulation, learn the R-value per inch. Knowing that, you can determine how many inches of a product is required to attain the total R-value that is recommended in your area. Attics should have more than walls because heat rises. That's good for all of us who are inspecting houses because attics are easy to inspect and, if need be, easier to insulate than walls. More and more states now require insulation for new construction. If you're buying a new house, check the building code in your area for the required amount, then check the house to learn if the insulation is up to code. But remember that building codes are usually minimum requirements. In my home I have more than is required in the attic, but I am convinced it pays to have it. Figure 27 shows one company's recommendations for R-value in the United States. These figures are not code requirements.

A typical wall is 3⅝ inches thick. That figure dictates the amount of insulation you can have in the wall. Different products, different value. Insu-

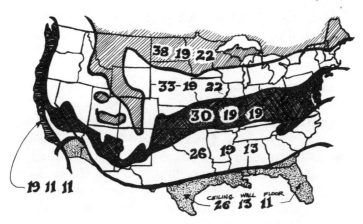

FIGURE 27. R-VALUES.

lating the walls of an existing house is difficult because of the anatomy of a wall. Usually it is done by drilling a few hundred holes through the exterior siding and pumping in the product. If it is not done correctly and thoroughly, you've wasted your money, and it's difficult to know whether all the spaces have been filled. When you consider that walls have diagonal bracing and fire stops (cats), you begin to understand the many honeycomblike voids there can be in a wall. It takes a plumb bob in the hands of a good worker to find and fill them all. Here again, reputable companies are important. One sure way of knowing that full insulation is added to a wall is to install new siding with an insulating backing. As a matter of fact, if the house you're buying has aluminum siding and you don't like the product, investigate closely before you tear it off. If it has Styrofoam backing, you'll be losing good insulation for your preference of wood over aluminum. I'm not criticizing your principles; I'm alerting your logic.

CEILINGS AND ROOFS: The ceiling or roof is the most important area to insulate. You lose more heat per square foot through uninsulated ceilings than you do through walls. Overall you lose more through walls because there's more wall area. But, as heat escapes through the ceiling, a draw effect is created. Cold air entering through uninsulated walls, floors, and poorly weather-stripped doors and windows is drawn ceilingward. Stopping the escape stops the draft. This can be done in several ways:

1. Stop infiltration of cold air around doors and windows. (A poorly weather-stripped house has the equivalent of one square foot of open space in a wall. Brrr! $$.)
2. Insulate the ceiling heavily.
3. Insulate floors, ceiling, and walls.

Alternative 3 is the most effective. In most areas of the United States it is the only solution. But if the house you're buying or living in has poor insulation in the walls, you can help greatly by doubling up on ceiling insulation and doing something about the floors. The cost is much less than insulating walls. And don't forget weather-stripping.

Houses that have no attic can be insulated. If rafters are exposed and the roof is good, you can consider adding insulation between the rafters and covering it with wood or gypsum board, leaving part of the rafters exposed. Or fill the entire area between the rafters and nail a new ceiling over the surface. If the roof is about gone (see Chapter 5), you can add insulation over the existing roof before applying the new waterproofing material. Thick shakes would have to be removed first. If it is a tar-and-gravel roof, rigid insulation is laid down on the existing roof, then plywood, then the new roof.

There are many new products being used for insulation. One is a urea foam applied in a continuous operation over the existing roof. This is a thick (1½-inch) white substance that is good insulation. However, it emits a formaldehydelike odor that has been known to cause nausea and other physical irritations in those who inhale it. The use of urea foam has been banned in most parts of the United States. If you suspect that a house has been insulated with urea foam, consult a professional home inspector. An excellent alternative to urea foam is cellulose insulation. Cellulose insulation is made up of pieces of wood and, like urea foam, is blown into the structure. Unlike urea foam, cellulose is completely harmless.

You hear and read much about insulating to save energy and money. It will do that, but let me tell you that the comfort achieved is just as valuable. In winter a well-insulated house does not have frequent and uncomfortable variables. The furnace rests longer between starts, and your body doesn't have to adjust so often. In summer, hot air is sealed out, and the air conditioning doesn't turn off and on so often.

Weather-stripping around doors and windows is important. Doors especially get rough treatment and get out of alignment. Flexible weather-stripping will take up the voids that occur when two solid pieces come together. Caulking around door and window frames is necessary. The wood on the exterior warps, shrinks, swells, and works, leaving cracks. Use a caulking compound that doesn't harden, for it will move with the working lumber and keep a seal. So check carefully for weather-stripping and good caulking. Stop infiltration.

If a house in an area of freezing winters doesn't have double-pane windows, there must be good storm windows. Triple pane is superior and should be considered if extensive remodeling is antici-pated. It's becoming common practice to install double-pane windows in newly built houses. It should be the code. If the house you are buying has the built-in quality mentioned above, you can ex-pect to pay for it, but you'll be happy you did.

Color is insulation also. Remember this: white re-flects heat, black attracts and lets heat go right through. Aluminum foil is a good reflector. Houses painted white inside make energy-saving sense in cold climates. In hot climates, white roofs and walls save much energy by reflecting heat that would otherwise have to be thrown off by air conditioning.

Check for smoke detectors. If there aren't any and you buy the house, add a few. Ask the fire de-partment for the best place to put them.

Solar Heat

If all the houses in the nation had solar collec-tors, the sun's energy would not be depleted by one BTU. It's that simple. The sun continually smiles at us and we ignore it.

Does the house you're inspecting have solar heat for water and/or space heating? A plus if it does. If not, consider it. After installing a solar hot-water system in our home, we actually feel that we are doing something meaningful about conservation. We recycle bottles and paper as many people do, but with solar heat we *see* the results. That helps. It's a good feeling to find that after taking a shower or washing the dishes the gas water heater did not operate. With 150-degree water going into our water heater, it didn't have to. What a satisfaction!

"How long will it be before it pays for itself?" we're often asked. We answer with a simple "Who cares?" One shouldn't always think about financial matters and whether the investment pays for itself. Think first whether the investment was wise. Hauling bottles and papers to the recycling depot is time, trouble, and expense, but it's the thing to do. Solar heating is also an investment in the future. They'll both pay in the long run, in more ways than one. If we live long enough, and the sun shines brightly enough, the system will pay for itself, but in the meantime it's great to have plugged in the sun. And while you're doing that, urge your representative in Congress to enact a good energy bill. Tell him or her that investing in the sun is a sure thing. It will always shine, but you have to be ready for it. Oil is expendable; sun is dependable.

Security

Security locks are important. Good ones are essential, or there is no security. Look at the door latch, which is the part that protrudes into the door jamb. If it has a small, half-round movable piece of metal on one side, you have a trigger bolt. That's better than a lock without one. The best lock is a dead bolt that requires a key from inside and out, both to lock and unlock. A mortise lock with buttons on the edge and a thumb turn on the inside is good, especially if the bolt is a long one. Short bolts are weak. Don't depend on a chain guard. Heavy snips can cut them with a snap.

Glass near a lock is not good, but if a dead-bolt lock is employed, the intruder could not reach in and unlock the door after breaking the glass. A key is required.

Glass sliding doors can be lifted out of the frame. A lock with a bolt set into a hole in the door frame is excellent. An alarm system is a bonus.

Windows are difficult. If you find steel bars covering windows and entrances, you've found a house either in a high-crime area or overprotective occupants. Look at neighboring houses. If doors and windows are heavily barred, it tells you something.

In any area a peephole on doors is helpful, as are exterior lights controlled from the bedroom. When in doubt, flick the switch. Better to be rude to indiscreet lovers than considerate to robbers.

Termites and Other Wood Destroyers 12

CONTRARY to popular belief, it doesn't take much knowledge to inspect for termites. There's nothing mysterious about them. They're as obvious as mud on a white wall. That was a "designed" metaphor, because mainly what we are looking for are mud tubes that subterranean termites build against the foundation as they search for wood. I believe a few words about those little creatures' habits will be a big asset in understanding what we're looking for during our inspection.

But first let me say that termites are tropical and prefer warm climates. In areas where winters are severe, termites are not common and not of great concern. My Wisconsin readers may want to skip this chapter, but my Georgia friends will need to read it. Houses in the northern states are not entirely exempt, however. The increasing use of central heat has made conditions quite comfortable for termites. So you people up there, check carefully around the furnace area for the signs of termites, which follow.

The common name for termites is white ants, but that's a misnomer because a termite is a worm. Ants and worms are a different order in the animal kingdom. Anyway, I like my friend's explanation better; he said they're called termites because if you leave them alone, they'll terminate your house.

Subterranean Termites

The kind that live in the earth (subterranean) are common in the United States and are the most destructive to houses. These termites do not expose themselves to the air, except in nuptial flights, but then they're only having fun, so who cares? Their colony is in the earth, but they live on wood. If there isn't food lying directly on the ground that they can reach from underneath, they build mud tubes up the foundation wall or the side of a pier, through which they can pass, gradually carrying your house with them. Everything eventually goes back to the earth anyway, so it's not surprising. The subterranean termite has to go back to the earth to get moisture to feed the bacteria that digest the wood he brought back with him. That's why he travels back and forth, and that's why he makes the tubes. Okay, so we look for tubes. Walk all around the exterior, pulling away brush and looking for dark brown mud lines about ¼ inch wide. If you see any, don't panic; the house isn't going to fall down on you. Stucco houses pose a problem because the stucco is often carried down the foundation to the earth. But stucco doesn't stick that close to concrete, and termites often crawl up between stucco and the foundation. No tubes are necessary.

This is worth repeating: subterranean termites live in the earth and they *do not* expose themselves to the air. This knowledge tells you that if you have no wood siding on the exterior of the house touch-

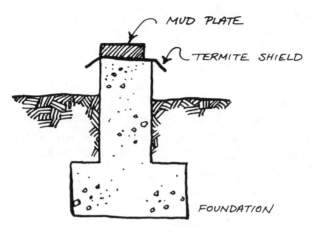

FIGURE 28. USING A TERMITE SHIELD.

ing earth, the only way termites can reach wood is
to build the tubes. If wood touches earth, no tubes
are necessary. If only two inches of concrete foundation are showing, it's enough. You can examine
the exterior nearly as fast as you can walk around
the perimeter. Besides the stucco situation mentioned above, termites can enter a house through
cracks in foundations.

In most eastern states metal termite shields are
used. Properly applied, the shield is installed between the mud plate and the foundation (Fig. 28).
It extends approximately two inches from the concrete on a 45-degree angle. If you find a shield,
check its condition. If it is rusted and deteriorated,
or flattened against the wall, it is undoubtedly useless. In a case like this it's better to depend on
poison.

Now put on your old clothes. A cap and gloves

are a help, for you should be as comfortable as possible so you'll stay beneath the house longer and do a good job. Have a strong, dependable flashlight so it won't go out on you when you get to the far reaches of that crawl space. Take a screwdriver and crawl in. Keep a sharp eye out. Shine your flashlight along the concrete, looking for tubes. Look also for freestanding tubes coming right out of the earth like an asparagus patch. If you see tubes, don't panic. Break them open and look for the small gray-white insects. If there are none, it probably means they have evacuated, but they could return, so destroy the tubes. If you find active termites, scrape away the tubes; the termites in the wood will die because you have prevented their access to the earth. Then test the wood all around the area where the tubes touched to determine if there is any damage. Poke hard; the wood may look sound, but it could be hollowed out inside. If so, it may be the cause of that sloping floor above. Have a professional carpenter determine the amount of damage and the costs to repair it, for this affects the value of the house. If you find a severe infestation, you may want to call in a pest control operator. After all, they are experts.

After destroying any tubes you've found, you can either get a good termiticide and spray the area yourself or have it done by a termite company. Most of it is not good material to breathe, so be careful. If you pour it into the earth next to the foundation from a small spout, it will prevent termites from building more tubes through the poisoned earth. Any of the pentachlorophenols are good termiticides. They are available under various trade names at building supply stores. Chlordane is also excellent.

You can see how important it is to have good earth-to-wood clearance. Without it, you cannot spot the tubes; where wood contact is direct, no tubes are necessary.

If you have seen termites swarming out of the earth next to your house, drying their new wings and flying away, it's a definite sign of infestation. You might think you're in luck that they're leaving. Not so. Only the winged reproductive termites swarm to set up a new colony. The workers and soldiers remain, trying to survive on your house. At this time of the year you might find the large swarming termites on windowsills or caught in spiderwebs. They're about ½ inch long, total length, with black-brown bodies and light gray wings. Or you might find just the wings. If so, it doesn't mean your house is infected. But it should alert you to look around for suspect areas of earth-to-wood contact, which would help them survive.

Subterranean termites get the most blame for damaging houses, and they deserve it. But there are other culprits too.

Dry-Wood Termites

The dry-wood termite is a slow-acting but determined creature, common in the South and Southwest. He likes redwood and oak and won't turn up his nose at any wood. He riddles the wood and shoves out small football-shaped pellets that are easily recognizable. You'll find the pellets along the baseboards or outside at the base of a wall, beneath floors, and especially in attics. Most of these creatures' damaging work is not seen. Once an invasion starts, it's best to tent the house and fumigate.

The damage from dry-wood termites generally occurs in the upper portions of a house. Attics are the best places to inspect. Look for football-shaped pellets. These termites live in the wood and need no earth contact. A general infestation would require tenting the house completely with plastic and inserting a poison gas: fumigation. Because this treatment leaves no residual protection, another infestation can occur. However, if the insects are only in a board or two, the area can be successfully treated locally with Paris green powder or penta. Both require holes bored in the wood to reach the galleries where the termites live.

Damp-Wood Termites

Another common termite is the damp-wood species. Larger than the other two, the damp-wood termite lives primarily in decaying wood but may move on to sound wood, provided it finds sufficient moisture. These termites are often found on decks, beneath bathrooms where faulty plumbing has decayed the wood, along eave lines, and in lumber stored on wet earth beneath a house. The ends of roof rafters are especially vulnerable. To control them, first get rid of the moisture, then the old wood, and finally treat the remaining wood with penta.

Ants or termites? They both have winged forms, and you'll see them come out of the earth and take wing, or you'll find them on windowsills. The differences are pronounced (Fig. 29). The ant has an

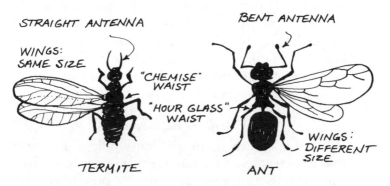

FIGURE 29. COMMON WOOD DESTROYERS.

"hourglass" waist, whereas the termite has a bulky "chemise" waist. The termite is not as delicate-looking, and neither is its action. The wings, too, are very different. The termite has four wings the same size; the ant's hind wings are smaller than its front ones. One more point: the ant's antennae are bent, the termite's straight.

Ants

Carpenter ants are big, shiny black, or black-and-red ants that make large, smooth galleries or chambers in wood. They don't actually feed on wood but hollow out nesting areas. Unlike a subterranean termite that consumes wood, leaving no trace, carpenter ants discard little shavings, or sawdustlike debris. Look around baseboards and other areas. Ants feed on kitchen wastes and can be seen searching for food. On warm spring days when they have other things in mind, carpenter ants grow wings and can be seen around windows trying to escape. If you see them, it's sometimes a sign that there is a colony somewhere in the house. Finding the nest is the problem. But treatment of the baseboards and other areas will weaken the colony and may discourage propagation. Dieldrin or chlordane emulsion is very effective.

Powder-Post Beetles

Another creature in the entomological world that does tremendous damage to a house but leaves conspicuous traces is the powder-post beetle. A good name, for it turns wood to powder. These beetles riddle the surface of wood with round holes that can make your entire basement or attic look as if it has been used as the backboard for a dart game. And you lost. The holes you see are emergence holes. When the larvae reach the adult stage, the beetles bore out, making the holes, but some eggs remain. It's the larvae that feed on wood, and by the time the holes appear, you've had several years of pupal development going on. When the subfloor gets riddled with tiny holes, the floor gets weak and springy. Strike the wood with your hand and you'll see powderlike dust fall out of the holes. Often you'll find the powder accumulated in little piles beneath infested lumber. These beetles get into furniture too, literally reducing an antique to a shell of its former self. Look in attics and basements mostly, although I've seen them everywhere. If the infestation is general, the best remedy is to fumigate. An effective local treatment is to apply deodorized kerosene mixed with 0.5 percent dieldrin or penta. But just as important as discovering any pest is determining how much damage they have done. That's what this inspection is all about. So once again, jab and pry at the infested lumber to ascertain how extensively it is weakened. Make a note. Enough of these notes and we may need a calculator.

The Old-House Borer

The old-house borer is the name for another wood-destroying insect. While the larvae are boring away, they make a rasping or ticking sound. You can hear them, but visual evidence comes only after much damage is done. When the adult leaves, there'll be ¼-inch broad oval holes in the wood.

Carpenter Bees

Carpenter bees are large black-and-yellow insects that look like bumblebees but have different habits. Carpenter bees bore into wood to make a home for their young. Look at porches, garages, sheds, railings, decks, roof overhangs, and outdoor furniture. The holes are ½ inch across, with galleries inside the wood, which make attractive nesting sites for the following year. An occasional hole won't weaken the wood, but enough of them will. The female, not the male, will sting. Most common insect aerosols are effective for control. Spray it in the holes, then plug them with putty. Do it after dark and you may not get stung.

Wood Rot

One important service termite inspectors offer is the search for dry rot. I've explained the nature and causes of this fungus, which I prefer to call wood rot. Dry rot is a misnomer. There's nothing dry about it. Certainly, it exists in dry weather, but it *had to have moisture* to grow. In fact, the fungus does not continue to grow when dry, but as soon as it picks up moisture, it becomes active. It destroys wood, leaving it soft and useless. Wood rot is found everywhere that the combination of wood, moisture, and airlessness exists. In your search for termite infestation, keep a sharp eye out for wood rot. Basements or crawl spaces are suspect; although they may be dry during your inspection and the fungus inactive, it will start again when moisture gathers during the winter and spring months.

Wood rot is very common. Look for it under eaves, around windows where putty cracks and allows water to seep in, or on decks, especially the joists where the decking lies, as well as between wood and concrete, at the end of supporting posts where they meet the concrete piers or foundations, and beneath bathrooms. Remember: MOISTURE ON WOOD WHERE NO AIR CIRCULATES PRODUCES WOOD ROT. If you find concrete over a wooden deck, check the wood carefully; use a small screwdriver and test the wood. Beneath decks, houses, and carports you can express yourself a little, but if it's finish lumber, such as window sash, be careful. Sometimes you see white fungus growing on wood, and often the wood becomes swollen. In that case the wood is soft for several inches. Whenever you see dark spots on wood be suspicious.

If you find minor wood rot and can prevent further moisture from reaching it, a good fungicide painted on the infected wood will stop the growth of fungus. But if the damage is severe enough to have weakened the wood so that it is no longer doing what it was intended to do, then that piece of wood will have to be replaced. Unfortunately, this usually occurs in hard-to-reach places, which makes the job slower and therefore more costly if you have to have it done.

We said above that if the lumber was weakened severely it would have to be replaced. That's true only if that wood is used to support part of the house, or if you walk on it (i.e., on a floor or deck). Sometimes you'll find wood rot on window sashes, deck railings, door and window trim, and often only a small amount beneath bathrooms, sinks, porches, steps, or around the baseboard in bathrooms. For cases like that there are some good products on the market. One is an epoxy substance that, when inserted into the rotted wood, will be absorbed, fill all deteriorated fibers, and cling fast to good wood. When dried, it is hard and permanent. It can be drilled, sanded, and painted. Don't ask termite inspectors about it because they like to think it doesn't exist, but boat owners know more about wood rot than anyone, and they use it. Ship chandlers carry the product, as do many hardware and supply houses. Ask for Rot-cure, Git-rot, Calignum, or something similar. Take advantage of science, but don't forget common sense.

Any wood stored beneath a house must be kept a good distance from the earth; otherwise you are inviting termites and providing their sustenance.

I have a running quarrel with termite inspectors when they report finding "cellulose debris" beneath a house. This frightens people into thinking a strange disease has attacked the property and, if it isn't remedied immediately, the house will crumble. It is an imposing phrase, but it's simply loose pieces of wood lying on the earth beneath the house, often left by the builder. It doesn't have to be diseased to warrant the phrase, but usually it is. It's still wood rot, but if it's lying loose, it gets the fancy name. If wood is fungus-infected and attached to the house, it's called dry rot.

All scraps of wood should be removed; they may be only scraps to you, but they're a feast to a termite. Also, while looking at the foundation or piers, you may see old form lumber left against the concrete, usually down low or in hard-to-reach places. That's why it's there; it was difficult for the builder to get out. It should be removed, or treated with penta.

If there's a concrete patio with screed boards (wooden separators), and the boards touch the walls of the house, it's potential trouble. The boards should be cut off two inches from the house and the space filled with concrete.

Respect termites but don't fear them. Remember, too, that termites and powder-post beetles have no more respect for a handmade house of distinction than for a prefab, tract ticky-tacky, or other zip-zap conformer. Sure, they do damage, but I've never known a house to fall down because of termite infestation. Follow the five rules on the next page and relax.

1. Use your head.
2. Keep moisture out of places where it shouldn't be.
3. Keep earth away from wood.
4. Make periodic inspections.
5. Apply chemicals around foundations.

Good luck.

13 How to Interpret a Termite Report

FIGURE 30 is a replica of a California termite report. They're not much different in other states. I chose California because infestation by all three kinds of termite is common there. Listed in the squares at the top are the various faults that could be found on the property, but only those marked with an X indicate which ones were discovered. Let's go through them and see what was found, and define the terms.

Subterranean termites were found, but no drywood termites. Next fungus, or dry rot, was found, but fortunately no powder-post beetles. Then comes faulty-grade level, which is checked. The term should be "faulty earth level," which means that the distance between earth and wood was not great enough. Most states require two inches of foundation above the earth on the exterior. Next is earth-to-wood contact, and this, as you know, is prohibited. No damp-wood termites were found. The shower leaks; this would be a stall shower, separate from the tub. No cellulose debris was found. Nor was there excessive moisture, so drainage was good. However, there are inaccessible areas. This is important. Because this area was in-

STANDARD STRUCTURAL PEST CONTROL INSPECTION REPORT
(WOOD-DESTROYING PESTS OR ORGANISMS)
This is an inspection report only - not a Notice of Completion.

ADDRESS OF PROPERTY INSPECTED	BLDG. NO. 27	STREET LOMITA	CITY Mill Valley, CA CO. CODE	DATE OF INSPECTION 9/26/77

FIRM NAME AND ADDRESS

MORPHEUS TERMITE CONTROL
ALTO, CALIFORNIA

Affix stamp here on Board copy only

↓ A LICENSED PEST CONTROL ↓
↑ OPERATOR IS AN EXPERT IN ↑
HIS FIELD. ANY QUESTIONS
RELATIVE TO THIS REPORT
SHOULD BE REFERRED TO HIM.

FIRM LICENSE NO. 13	CO. REPORT NO. (if any) 726	STAMP NO. 1226

Inspection Ordered by (Name and Address) **Mark Twichell**
Report Sent to (Name and Address) **27 LOMITA, Mill Valley, CA.**
Owner's Name and Address **Pat Heyman**
Name and Address of a Party in Interest **Marlys Cheyne, 500 Wall Street, Seattle, Washington**
INSPECTED BY **Mark Hoffman**   LICENSE NO. **717**   Original Report ☒   Supplemental Report   Number of Pages

YES	CODE	SEE DIAGRAM BELOW	YES	CODE	SEE DIAGRAM BELOW	YES	CODE	SEE DIAGRAM BELOW	YES	CODE	SEE DIAGRAM BELOW
X	S-Subterranean Termites			B-Beetles-Other Wood Pests			Z-Dampwood Termites			EM-Excessive Moisture Condition	
	K-Dry-Wood Termites		X	FG-Faulty Grade Levels		X	SL-Shower Leaks			IA-Inaccessible Areas	
X	F-Fungus or Dry Rot		X	EC-Earth-wood Contacts			CD-Cellulose Debris		X	FI-Further Inspection Recom.	

1. SUBSTRUCTURE AREA (soil conditions, accessibility, etc.)   See below #1
2. Was Stall Shower water tested? **Yes**   Did floor coverings indicate leaks? **Yes**
3. FOUNDATIONS (Type, Relation to Grade, etc.) Concrete-F.G.   #4
4. PORCHES . . . STEPS . . . PATIOS   #3 and #4
5. VENTILATION (Amount, Relation to Grade, etc.)   Adequate
6. ABUTMENTS . . . Stucco walls, columns, arches, etc.   None
7. ATTIC SPACES (accessibility, insulation, etc.)   Not inspected
8. GARAGES (Type, accessibility, etc.)   None
9. OTHER

DIAGRAM AND EXPLANATION OF FINDINGS (This report is limited to structure or structures shown on diagram.)

General Description_____ Two and one half story rustic A-frame residence.

(1.) SUBSTRUCTURE: Sub-area, partially improved. Wooden platform is inaccessible on underside. Earth wood contact where dirt bank has fallen against the back wall. Evidence of termite infestation noted.

RECOMMENDATION: Remove wooden platform and saturate earth with a soil toxicant. Replace platform on masonry supports . Remove earth from back wall. Treat wood with approved chemical. Replace all infested wood with new wood.

(2.) SHOWER: Stall shower pan was tested according to prescribed method and was found to leak.

RECOMMENDATION: Remove shower pan and adjacent two rows of tiles. Install new shower pan. Replace bottom two rows of tile. Color match as close to existing tile as possible.

(2A) LOWER SHOWER: Lower shower is on concrete slab. No water test to pan was made as under area inaccessible. Rug near shower shows evidence of moisture. This due to improper sealing of shower door.

RECOMMENDATION: Replace shower door with new. Safety glass required. No replacement of rug allowed for in this report.

(3.) DECK: The posts supporting the deck exhibit fungus damage at the base. Some posts are imbedded in the soil.

RECOMMENDATION: Cut off the posts to good wood. Install masonry bases.

(4.) STEPS: Faulty grade level exists at base of front steps.

RECOMMENDATION: Remove earth to prescribed distance.

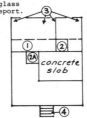

concrete
slab

FIGURE 30. A TERMITE REPORT.

accessible, it explains the last square: further inspection is necessary. Termite inspectors aren't required to remove boards and gain access to areas. If they can't get into a certain place and they feel it should be inspected, they recommend further inspection at additional cost.

Next on the report are nine categories that are self-explanatory. After that is a diagram of the house and garage, together with text explaining in detail where the faults were found and the recommendations to correct them. The numbers in the text refer to the numbers in the sketch. A cost sheet will also be included.

Termite Clearance

You've probably heard the term "termite clearance" and wondered what it meant. It means that a licensed termite inspector guarantees that the house is free of all infestations and meets the state specifications. Only a licensed inspector can give a clearance. In the case above, the cost to do the work was $1,400. A clearance would be issued by the company if the work was done according to their report. You don't have to hire the inspector to do the work before a clearance is issued. After you have a report, you have a guide; you can do the work yourself or hire a carpenter to do it. But it will take another inspection before the clearance can be issued. In some states it's not called a clearance but rather a certificate, which states the absence of termites or that treatment has been completed.

A growing number of loan agencies require a home buyer to have a clearance before any money is loaned on the property. In such a case, the loan company withholds the amount the termite company says it will cost to clear the property. Let's say it's $1,400. The loan company puts that amount in escrow. You move into the house and you have the termite report. It tells exactly what has to be done to clear the property. If you can do the work yourself, so much the better. If you want to gamble, hire another company for another opinion. You may save yourself some money. There's frequently a big difference in opinions. Some inspectors are more lenient than others, some more careless, and some can see a much easier way of correcting faults, which makes the job less costly. Or ask your agent to recommend good contractors or carpenters who could do the work. Any agent who is worth his or her salt has a list of workers who are capable and who understand termite work. After the work is done, you hire a licensed inspector to check the work and, we hope, grant a clearance. Then the escrow company will release the $1,400. In many cases the company will release the money on a guarantee from a contractor.

In all cases I suggest you talk with the original inspector before doing anything. Explain your circumstances. Frequently they'll show you what portion of the work you can do yourself, leaving the more difficult and sophisticated jobs for them. Removing earth is work; it won't hurt you to do it. If you do level with the inspector and he isn't helpful, get another one. You shouldn't deal with uncooperative people anyway. Don't worry that he will alert other inspectors to refuse you a clearance. There's so much competition in this business that you can easily get another inspector to examine your job and issue a clearance. Remember to watch out for "sweetheart arrangements."

Let's take a case where you don't need a clearance. In your agreement the seller will pay a thousand dollars toward termite work. The report shows faulty grade level, some dry rot, termites in one corner, and excessive moisture in the crawl space beneath the floor. You now know how to take care of those things and you're not lazy. Tell your agent you want the thousand dollars. The agreement doesn't stipulate the money has to go to a termite company. Put it in the bank and let it draw interest while you're working around the house.

In nearly all cases the buyer pays for the inspection report. You might be buying a house "as is." The seller will not pay anything toward repair work. He can do that. Most states do not require a termite inspection. But that doesn't stop you from getting one. After it arrives, I urge you to study it closely and to check it against the house to learn if the assertions made are accurate. If you have doubts, call the inspector. Make him prove them. Keep in mind that as a rule termite inspectors are looking for work. They are contractors who make a living doing repairs, not doing inspections. I know some who are fair and honest. I hope you can find one.

Needless to say, if the house is infested with dry-wood termites or powder-post beetles and has to be tented and fumigated, that's not a do-it-yourself project. But get several bids for the job.

Now a word in defense of termite inspectors.

The criticism most frequently heard is that they

are too strict, especially on old houses that were built before so much was known about infestations and how to avoid them. Many recent building codes require termite prevention, so houses built before the new laws were written contain many violations of the present codes. Can old houses be exempt, as they are for, say, electric wiring? No. This is one case where the laws are retroactive. So don't blame the inspector. He has to report all violations of the present state pest control board specifications on old houses as well as new. But it's a two-way street. If you're buying, you want a strict report; if you're selling, you may complain.

14 How to Make an Offer

ARMED with your ability and the knowledge you have gained from this book, I hope you have enough confidence to inspect a house for yourself. And you should be able to ask more knowledgeable questions of the seller or the agent you are dealing with. Remember, too, if you like your agent, stay with him or her. Some people think that only the agent whose name is on the "For Sale" sign can sell the house. This is generally not so. Respected agents cooperate. So even though one agent has the listing, he or she will usually allow others to sell the house.

Contrary to what some people say, an agent does perform many valuable services, which I think you should be made aware of.

One: he (or she) carefully selects houses for you to look at that suit your needs, thus saving you hours and days of useless running around by yourself. He has listings of what is on the market, with information on the number of rooms, baths, proximity to schools, class of neighborhood, zoning, taxes, appraised value, and so on. Two: he arranges financing. This is important, for he has contact with lending agencies, and if he is well respected, the agency will often bend the rules and make a loan on a house that they might not consider otherwise. A good agent tries harder, for he needs the commission. Three: he arranges for termite inspections and any repairs needed. Four: he acts as the negotiator between buyer and seller. He does the haggling for you. If you're not good at such confrontations, this can be a very uncomfortable experience. Some people enjoy it, but most do not. Know thyself!

Contracts

Finally we come to writing a contract. This is perhaps the point of mystery most feared and respected by a buyer. Most people feel a lawyer is a necessity here. In some states an agent can write the contract, but this may not be wise if he or she is also working for, and being paid by, the seller. The contract gets the ball rolling, and that's what you want. The contract will name a title insurance company and an escrow agent to handle that business. Or you can name the companies you wish. And the contract will list all conditions of sale. If the contract is agreeable to both parties, the signatures are gathered, a deposit is made, and the agent or attorney then seeks financing. When that is approved, the contract goes to the escrow agent, where many details will be handled. When all conditions are satisfied, the escrow company will return the final papers to the agent and all of the details will be explained to the buyer and seller, and the deal is then finalized.

But supposing you don't want to use an agent or lawyer; you want to buy directly from the seller. You're an adult, you can negotiate a loan. Once you and the seller come to an agreement, all you need is an escrow agent and perhaps a title insurance company. But before you open an escrow account, you've got to read the rest of this chapter, for there are many things you should know about the house. Here are a few of them.

You've already run yourself ragged and found the house you like; you're ready to start talking business. You've only been through the house and have yet to make your inspection. But there are other facts and figures you should know about before you make your offer, in order to determine whether or not you can afford the costs of purchasing and maintaining the house.

1. How much are the taxes per year?
2. What is the tax rate per hundred assessed evaluation?
3. How much is the house assessed for?
4. When was it last assessed?
5. How much do utilities cost per month? Ask to see receipts.
6. How much will you have to borrow? Then ask a loan company how much the payments are per month on that amount, for twenty-five or thirty years at the going rate of interest. How much are closing costs?
7. How much is insurance?
8. What is the cost of upkeep? This is difficult to determine precisely, but there are always some repairs.

Assessed versus Appraised Values

After you've added up these figures, you're in a better position to know if you can afford the house.

There's a difference between assessed and appraised value. Assessed value is a percentage of appraised value, and the amount of that percentage varies from state to state and often from county to county, but the confusion is about the same. Appraised value is market value. Assessed value is taxation value. Your taxes are computed at so much per hundred assessed value. When you phone the assessor's office to learn the assessed value, ask what percentage that is of the appraised, or market, value. Don't hesitate to call. This is public knowledge. They'll give it to you. Another thing to find out from local residents is whether there is a pending change in assessment policy, and how school taxes affect assessment. This could affect your tax bill substantially.

When you know what the house is assessed for, it is a good yardstick as to the value of the house. At least you know whether it is far overpriced. Assessors are supposed to assess at fair market value, but sometimes they are not up to date and prices can change quickly, depending upon the market in certain areas. Generally, houses do sell for more than the appraised value. The assessor's office may tell you the average percent of selling price over appraised value.

If, for example, you pay $80,000 for a house that is appraised for $60,000, your taxes will undoubtedly be increased within a year because the assessor will know what you paid; the market value went up.

This will make a difference in your monthly costs. The law is changing in several states. Property taxes will simply be a certain percentage of the market value, plus adjustments for special districts.

Pest Reports

Ask the seller if he has had a termite inspection. If he has, learn the date and whether the work was done. Ask to see the report. If he has no report, but you know the house was inspected in the last five years, in most states you can get a copy of the report for two dollars from the state pest control board. If you have a report, you can easily check it to see if the work has been done. If, on the other hand, he shows you a report of an inspection and a clearance, which is proof that the work has been done, and it was within the past two years, you can be quite certain the structure is free of infestation. If it was any longer ago than that, ask if he is going to have an inspection. He may say no. Then it's up to you. If, after you have made your own inspection, you are not confident about the termite situation, you must decide whether you want to order a professional inspection. As I said, some loan companies require a clearance before they will loan on a house. But even though the seller is not going to pay anything toward termite work, he'll allow you to have an inspection if you pay for it. Ask around. In some states the rule is that the seller pays for a termite report and the results are negotiable. In others the buyer pays for the report and the seller does the work. Ordinarily it is not a case of law but of custom. The real estate boards in your area will tell you the normal procedure.

Public Files

Before you make an offer, go to the building and planning department of city hall. Ask if they have a file on the property. This is public knowledge also. Study the file. Anything you find is important; the file will show if building permits have been issued and what they were for. Sometimes the record shows when a roof was installed, or a water heater, deck, or second bath. In addition, it will tell you whether an inspection was made on the room that was added to the house you want to buy. The seller may brag about the room, but was it done to code? Perhaps it was, but if no permit was issued, you know the building inspector didn't see the job.

You may find that all the facts on the file are favorable. In that case you'll have peace of mind. But check for the zoning classification for the area: single family, duplex, multiple? Learn what the side-yard setback requirements are, and determine if the house conforms to the ordinances. Mainly you want to learn if there are any restrictions, such as variances, which would make the house noncon-forming. It could be a duplex, for example, but new zoning has made the area single family, R-1. In that case you would have a legal nonconforming use. That's not critical, but you should know it because any encumbrance makes the property harder to sell and makes it more difficult to get permission for improvements. If the house is on a steep hill-side, ask if the foundation was engineered. Most communities require it, depending upon the slope. If blueprints are available, all the better. Examine them, but remember, the map is not the territory;

blueprints don't guarantee that the house was built according to the plans.

All right, so no agent is involved. In this case the seller will undoubtedly know the procedure, but for your own protection you'd better be aware of how it's done. The seller has his interests; you have yours. Books have been written explaining how to sell your home without using an agent or broker, describing step by step what escrow agents and title insurance companies do for the seller and buyer, but actually their duties are so routine it's hardly worth a chapter. This is not to say they are not important; they have their place in our society. They are convenient and perform important jobs that are mysterious to most people. We have to live with them, so a brief explanation of their duties is in order.

Escrow

Escrow simply means a set of instructions given to a third party (escrow company) to hold with your deposit until the conditions described in those instructions are met. For example: an escrow company will prorate taxes and fire insurance, see that the title is recorded for county records, pay off all trust deeds and mortgages, if any, withhold its fee, and pay the title insurance company, etc. All of these disbursements will be explained to both buyer and seller, as mentioned.

Title Insurance

Title insurance is entirely different. The enduring nature of land makes it possible for several parties to claim rights to a piece of property. The claims could include an easement (right of way) across the land, an old judgment, an unpaid mortgage, a lien against the property, and many others. A title company makes a search of all available records to determine the soundness of the land title. If anything untoward is discovered, these findings will be revealed to you. In the event the title company feels there is clear title to the property, it will issue title insurance (for a fee) to protect you, the buyer, against title hazards. This insurance covers you for legal defense against an attack on a title by someone who believes that he has a claim to the property.

Very few states have a law making it mandatory that a buyer purchase title insurance. They don't force you to insure personal property from theft. It's up to you. But if you have to borrow money to buy the property, loan companies have a rule that you must insure the title. After all, it's really their house until the loan is paid off and they want it insured, at your expense naturally. I certainly don't advocate skipping title insurance in any case. Ask what the costs are, then decide if the service and assurance are worth the price. There's nothing stopping you from making your own title search. County records are open to the public, so it is quite simple to search those records to learn if any mechanics' liens or encumbrances have been recorded. If you find none, and you feel absolutely safe that no heir can claim the property you wish to purchase, then skip the insurance, save the insurance costs, and buy the property.

The procedure for buying property without an agent differs from state to state, and sometimes within a state. In northern California, for example, most title insurance companies may also act as escrow agents if they are licensed to do so. In southern California the rule is that escrow companies are separate from title companies, but the trend is to combine them. Because rules vary from area to area and are also changing, it would be useless to describe what the procedure is now in the various states.

The best advice I can give you, the buyer, is to go to a title insurance company, or an escrow company, and tell them you are going to purchase a home without using an agent. Ask what the costs are, if you want them to handle it, and what the procedure is. They will be very helpful. It's their business to handle transactions like this.

But no matter what the procedure is in your particular area, it must be remembered that title insurance companies and escrow agents are disinterested third parties to any transaction. That is, there must be total agreement between seller and buyer as to price and conditions before you go to the company to start proceedings for the final sale. They will not do any haggling for you.

In all probability, you will be told to get a "contract for the purchase of real estate and receipt of deposit." Easy. Almost all stationery stores carry them, as do some title companies. You and the seller will get together and fill it out. You will make a deposit at this time, which will be returned to you if the conditions listed on the form are not met. And now we come to the most important part of your offer. Conditions.

For example, (1) this offer is subject to a house

inspection by yourself or by a professional if you wish. (This clause will protect you if you find serious faults and the seller won't correct them or pay for them.) (2) Financing. You already know how much you have to borrow, so your offer could be subject to getting a loan of a certain amount on the house, at a certain rate of interest. These figures will be precise when you know them. (3) You may want the stove and the refrigerator, drapes, washer and dryer, carpets, chandeliers, mirrors; if so, make all these items a condition. (4) If you want a professional termite inspection, make that a condition. Sometimes the seller agrees to pay up to a certain amount toward termite work. If that is the case, be sure and state that amount in the agreement. (5) You may want assurance that all appliances be kept in working order until the close of escrow. And to protect the seller, and give you some working time, you can stipulate that you will satisfy the conditions within ten or twenty days. Before you sign, you might want an attorney to check the papers. If you and the seller sign, you have a preliminary agreement and the house is off the market. Remember too that if you are purchasing through an agent, you can insist on the above conditions, and more if you think of them.

Now it's up to you to begin satisfying the conditions. I suggest you start with financing, for while the loaning institution is doing their work, you can be doing yours. Take this book with you and give the house a thorough inspection. When you get through, you'll know a lot more about the house than if you had taken an agent's word for it.

Suppose you find serious faults in the house, but

you would still like to buy it. Show the faults to the seller and tell him you'll buy the house provided he does the repairs or has them done. Or, if you are handy and don't mind the work, tell the seller you'll purchase minus the amount you think it will cost to make repairs. And don't forget the termite report. If there is infestation, you'll have to come to an agreement with the seller. If the seller is adamant and won't cooperate, tell him you don't want the house and go find another one. But don't forget your deposit.

One thing is certain: it's better to lose a bad house because of your knowledge than to gain one through ignorance. Too many unwary buyers fall into the latter category.

If you have engaged an agent, and you or a private inspector found serious faults on the property, the agent will then confront the seller with the facts. If you still like the house, you will ask that the faults be corrected or a sufficient amount of money be deducted to have them repaired. If the seller refuses to cooperate and makes a statement to the effect that he'll sell to someone else, your agent must tell the seller that under the full disclosure law, which most states have, he, the agent, must inform all prospective buyers about any known faults. It's a law to help consumers. The listing agent must be informed, and it would be fraudulent for the seller to withhold known information. Usually sellers cooperate; and if the agent is firm in his convictions, he will reveal all known faults. The seller realizes he may as well cooperate with you as with someone else.

Back to the direct sale. When you and the seller

agree ʌthat all conditions have been met, you will open escrow proceedings. Now there's very little chance the deal will not go through. When the time for closing of escrow has arrived, you and the seller will be notified and you and your attorneys, if hired, meet at the escrow company. It may be required that you have an attorney present. There all the figures and disbursements of money will be read and explained to you. If all is in order, the deed to the property will be signed over to you. You've bought yourself a house.

I hope I've helped. Your next step should be to consider homesteading your property. Most states allow this, and rightly so. In this country the tradition is that every person deserves a place to live. The law varies in different states, but essentially homesteading protects the homeowner from being wiped out completely by some calamity—a lawsuit, an illness, or some other misfortune. In California, for example, homestead exemptions apply up to $20,000 if you are married, $10,000 if you are single. This means that if a judgment is obtained against a homeowner over a lawsuit, an accident, medical costs, or the like, he or she would be protected for the amount listed. There are some exemptions, such as mechanics' liens and mortgages. If you don't make your payments, the mortgage company can foreclose and take your property, sell it, and keep what you owe them. But whatever is left over is protected from other creditors if your property is legally homesteaded.

The homestead law is very lenient "way out west," but they can afford it. Most states do very little for homesteading. Check it out. The county clerk knows about it, or ask an attorney. You may find that you can get a form for homesteading in a stationery store, fill it out, have it notarized, and for a small fee have it recorded in the county records. I did. I strongly advise your investigating homesteading. After all, laws are made to be used, not abused.

Your Semiannual Maintenance Schedule 15

KEEPING your house in shape is simply a matter of paying attention to problems and fixing them before they get out of control. Spending just an hour or two inspecting your home each spring and fall will keep you from expensive repairs in summer and winter.

When making these inspections, having a checklist will keep you from overlooking some simple but potentially costly problems. By using the simple checklist that follows (and healing the wounds of your aging home as quickly as possible), you can add years of life to your house and save hundreds of dollars on repairs and possibly thousands of dollars in replacement costs.

The Fall Maintenance Schedule

When doing seasonal maintenance inspections, bear in mind that your task is twofold. First, you are inspecting for damage and wear and tear from the previous season. Second, you are preparing the house for the coming season. In all seasons you'll want to give the house a quick inspection from foundation to roof just to check for problems.

Fall is the time to batten down the hatches. You

want to make sure your house is ready for the coming cold. Start in your basement or cellar and work your way up through the house. Pay particular attention to your gutters—they'll need cleaning.

INTERIOR: Begin by inspecting both the interior and exterior foundation for cracks or voids. These are an open invitation for excess water as well as rodents and insects. Should you see any signs of moisture, you have reason to suspect a leak in the foundation. Be sure to patch any of the cracks or holes that you find.

While you are downstairs, give your heating system the once-over. If you have a steam heating system, this means bringing up the level of water. If you use oil, you should check your fuel supply and clean your furnace air filters.

At this time you should be tightening up around windows and doors to prevent unnecessary heat loss. Check your entry doors and storm doors to make sure they are operating properly and are weathertight. Replace all your screen windows and doors with storm windows and doors. Check to see that your windows and storm windows are not cracked. Then replace all your screen windows and doors with storm windows and doors. If your windows have sash cords, look to see that they are not broken. Be sure that the putty seal surrounding the windows is intact.

Fall Maintenance Schedule: Interior
_____ Patch cracks in foundation.
_____ Check dryness.

_____ Test furnace (schedule a tune-up).

_____ Replace or clean air filters in furnace.

_____ Check all fluid levels of heating system.

Water level   ☐ empty ☐ half ☐ full

Oil level   ☐ empty ☐ half ☐ full

_____ Insulate basement windows.

_____ Replace screen windows and doors with storm windows and doors.

_____ Check all windows for cracks.

_____ Check sash cords.

_____ Check putty seal.

_____ Make sure all doors are working properly.

_____ Make sure all windows and doors are weathertight.

EXTERIOR: No matter what climate you may live in, fall is an ideal time of year to do exterior painting. The humidity is low, the temperature is bearable, and rainfall is only intermittent. It is also a good time to check your gutters. All gutters should be cleaned thoroughly. If your gutters are made of wood, be sure to oil them as well. The oil will preserve the wood and will prevent them from clogging. It will also deter the eventual backflow of rainwater and the possibility of ice damming up under the roof shingles. Aluminum gutters should be checked for rust buildup.

While you are cleaning the gutters, check the condition of the roof. It is important to do this well before the colder and wetter months set in, as any necessary repairs must be done before the bad weather. Check to see that the shingles are holding strong and that there are no cracks, holes, or soft spots.

Remember to check the exterior foundation for cracks and voids.

Fall Maintenance Schedule: Exterior

____ Do any exterior painting or staining that is necessary.

____ Clean and oil gutters when necessary.

____ Check the roof.

____ Check the foundation for cracks and voids.

The Spring Maintenance Schedule

If fall is the time to batten down for the cold, spring is the time to prepare for the coming summer. You will notice that many of the maintenance procedures are similar to those done in the fall—cleaning the gutters and heating system, for example. Yet, in some instances, you actually will have to "undo" what you did in the fall.

INTERIOR: Again, begin in the basement. You should reexamine the foundation as cracks or voids may develop as a result of a particularly cold or stormy winter. Examine your plumbing system as well to make sure there are no leaks. While you are still in the basement, take time to clean your heating unit. If your heating system is run on steam, this is the time of year it must be drained.

Before replacing your storm windows and doors

with screens, be certain to check them thoroughly. Make sure there are no cracks in the windows and no caulking problems. Lubricate all metal hinges and clasps around the windows and doors (and cupboards as well). You might want to soap the window edges and sashes to ease movement of the window.

The availability of fresh air makes this a good time for interior painting, papering, or floor refinishing. The breezes can diffuse the otherwise toxic fumes.

For those of you with a fireplace, this is the time of year to have a professional chimney sweep clean your chimney. You can help by cleaning the fireplace itself.

Spring Maintenance Schedule: Interior

_____ Patch cracks in foundation.

_____ Check dryness.

_____ Make sure there are no leaks in the plumbing.

_____ Clean or drain the heating system.

_____ Replace the storm windows and doors with screen windows and doors.

_____ Check windows and caulking for cracks.

_____ Lubricate all metal hinges and clasps.

_____ Do any necessary interior painting, papering, or refinishing.

_____ Clean chimney and fireplace.

EXTERIOR: Spring is the time to think about the exterior of your home. For example, are you considering doing any landscaping or gardening? Soil is soft in the spring, and new gardens can be dug very easily. You also may need to do some pruning where the winter's winds have torn down branches and the like.

Carefully check your porch and railings for dry rot or excessive wear. While walking around the outside of your house, make sure that your downspouts are in place and that none are missing. This leads us to the gutters. Once again, check to see that your gutters are clean. You should go up to the roof to see that no twigs or branches have fallen into the gutters. Also, carefully examine the roof. Make sure that there are no holes or leaks or soft spots. Finally, take a look at the siding on the house. Determine whether you will need to do any repainting, staining, or siding before the next winter.

Spring Maintenance Schedule: Exterior

____ Check exterior foundation for cracks or voids.

____ Plan and prepare ground for landscaping or gardening.

____ Clear away all branches or twigs thrown about in winter storms.

____ Check porch and railings for dry rot and wear.

_____ See that the roof is in good condition.

_____ Clean gutters.

_____ Check exterior siding.

Condominiums

IN GENERAL this book applies to all kinds of buildings, whether single family or multiple. But because condominiums are growing in popularity I
would like to offer a few words of caution to persons seeking that type of housing. Group living
makes sense in areas where land values are high,
but we all need privacy to keep our senses.

Aside from the overall construction of the building, the single most important aspect of condomin-
ium living is soundproofing. If the building is fifteen years old or more, be very careful about
checking into sound. Light classical music doesn't
mix well with hard rock. Spend some time in the
apartment while occupants are home, both alongside and overhead. Listen carefully for sounds in
water pipes, steps overhead, doors closing, hi-fi,
and street traffic. The last is important, especially
for night ventilation, so open a window and listen
for street noises.

The newer buildings have double-wall construction, and insulation is almost always used, so
sounds seldom come through walls from adjoining
apartments. But it is much harder to insulate be-

tween floors, so pay attention to that important detail.

Following are some other points to consider while shopping for group living.

Heating: If there is central heat, do you have positive individual control? You don't want to be governed by someone else's idea of comfort. How is the cost divided? And who pays for upkeep and cost of repair? Forced-air furnaces are common, and some of them are noisy. If there's a furnace for each unit, turn it on and check for noise. Some of them emit a whoosh of air that continues all the time the fan is on. The fan noise can be distracting.

Plumbing: Are there individual hot-water heaters or is there a general source that is supposed to provide enough to go around? If from a general source, who pays costs and upkeep? Are costs shared equally regardless of family size? If there are two of you and families of four in other units, that's a consideration. How is general maintenance handled?

Parking: How is the security for all-night parking? What arrangements are there for guests, yours and others? Are cars starting their motors and testing their carburetors early in the morning going to bother you?

Security: Is there good lighting from the parking area to your door? Are corridors well lighted?

Fire: Are there fire extinguishers and smoke detectors in hallways and corridors? Better have smoke detectors in your own unit also.

Swimming guests: Can you invite all the friends you wish to come and swim? If so, remember that other owners have the same privilege. Think about it.

Decks: Concrete decks over wood often are troublesome. Concrete is not waterproof. There must be a good waterproofing agent between the concrete and the wood beneath. You can't see it, so try and get beneath the deck and look for water stains. If you see any, beware. It could mean wood rot. Perhaps the owners will take care of it, but it is best to avoid buying trouble.

Repairs: You are responsible for your own apartment, but what if, for example, a plumbing leak from above occurs? Your ceiling is ruined. Whose responsibility is it and who pays for your repair? Is it entirely up to you to take care of the problem?

Besides the physical aspects mentioned, I cannot stress too much that you thoroughly understand the legal document you sign, which should clearly specify your commitment and also the association's responsibilities. If you are in any doubt about even the smallest detail, ask questions and understand the answers. Or engage an attorney to check it.

Is there a management firm that takes care of the grounds, pool, and other general maintenance? Do you have a vote in the management policy? Ask about an owners' association, and if there is one, learn how it functions. Think, too, that, generally speaking, the larger the association the smaller your voice. Leave nothing to chance. Simply keep in mind that this will be your home, your shelter. Don't be a victim of those famous last words after it's too late: "You signed the agreement."

Inspection Checklist
for Quick Reference

THE following checklist is a valuable tool not only for buyers but also for homeowners. The procedures are structured so as to take you through a house in the same thorough and efficient manner that professional home inspectors use. The more complex features whose function affects the house as a whole are listed separately for your convenience.

Before you begin the actual inspection, be sure to make note of the following items.

What type of **fuel** is used? _____
What is the approximate **age** of the house? _____
Approximately how much fuel will be used during
    the colder months? $ ____ units ____
    Does this include cooking? ____
    Use of the hot-water heater? ____

Exterior

What is the exterior? **paint** ____ **stain** ____
  stone ____ **cement** ____ other ____
What is the condition of the exterior?
  cracking ____ checking ____ peeling ____

Is the exterior made of **aluminum siding?** ____

    Is the siding firm? ____ loose? ____

    Will you need to replace it?

    yes ____ no ____

In what condition is the **window trim?**

    good ____ fair ____

    Will you need to scrape and paint it?

    yes ____ no ____

    Will you need to replace it?

    yes ____ no ____

Is the **putty** serviceable? yes ____ no ____

    Is it cracked? yes ____ no ____

    Does it need replacing? yes ____ no ____

Is the **caulking** serviceable? yes ____ no ____

Check the **molding** in all corners, doorways, and

    windows. Does any of it need renailing?

    yes ____ no ____

    If so, where? _____

    Does any of it need replacement?

    yes ____ no ____

    If so, where? _____

Are the **gutters** made of wood?

    yes ____ no ____

    Or are they galvanized? yes ____ no ____

    Will you need to repair or replace them?

    yes ____ no ____

What are the conditions of the **chimneys** and

    vents? good ____ fair ____ poor ____

Drainage

What are the **gutters** made of?

wood ____ aluminum ____

If they are wood, when was the last time they were oiled? _____

If they are aluminum, are they rusty?

yes ____ no ____

Are the gutters clear and clean?

yes ____ no ____

Are there any **downspouts?** yes ____ no ____

What condition are they in?

good ____ rusty ____

Where do they drain into? _____

Does the water flow *away* from the
house? ____

Or does the water settle into the
foundation? ____

Is there a **leader drain?** yes ____ no ____

What condition is it in?

good ____ rusty ____

Roof

What kind of roof is it? **tar and gravel** ____

wood shingles ____ **shakes** ____

asphalt shingles ____ **slate** ____ other ____

What kind of condition is the roof in?

good ____ fair ____ poor ____

What kind of condition are the **ridges** in?

  good _____ fair _____ poor _____

What kind of condition are the **valleys** in?

  good _____ fair _____ poor _____

What kind of condition are the **flashings** in?

  good _____ fair _____ poor _____

*Are there **snow guards?**   yes _____ no _____

*Is there an **ice dam barrier?**   yes _____ no _____

  *This item may not be necessary in every climate.

Attic Area

Is there any evidence of roof leaks?

  yes _____ no _____

Is the attic properly ventilated?

  yes _____ no _____

Is the attic insulated?   yes _____ no _____

Is it accessible to insulate?   yes _____ no _____

What is the size of the **roof rafters?** _____

  Are the rafters properly spaced?

  yes _____ no _____

Is there any evidence of sagging?

  yes _____ no _____

Are there **collar beams** (bracing)?

  yes _____ no _____

  Is there a knee wall?   yes _____ no _____

Are the **floor joists** spaced properly?

  yes _____ no _____

What is the length of the span between the **bearing walls?** _____

Is there any evidence of sagging here?

yes _____ no _____

Is there **flooring material?**

yes _____ no _____ partial _____

Is there evidence of the existence of **ice dams?**

yes _____ no _____

Are there **hurricane ties?** yes _____ no _____

Electric

What is the **service size?** _____

What is the number of **amperes?** _____

What is the number of **circuits?** _____

Are there 230 volts or 115 volts? _____

Is there a **main disconnect?** yes _____ no _____

What is the number of **circuit breakers?** _____

What is the number of **fuses?** _____

Are the circuits overfused? yes _____ no _____

Are there appliance circuits in the kitchen?

yes _____ no _____

Is the wiring adequate? yes _____ no _____

Will you need to do rewiring?

yes _____ no _____

partial rewiring? yes _____ no _____

Are there 230 volt outlets? yes _____ no _____

Heating

What type of **heating system** does the house have?

forced air _____ gravity _____ electric _____

hot water _____ radiant _____ oil _____

gas _____ other _____

Do the heating controls work?

yes _____ no _____

Is the **combustion chamber** clean?

yes _____ no _____

Will the heating unit need cleaning to improve
efficiency?   yes _____ no _____

What is the number of **BTUs?** _____

If the heating unit is forced air, is the motor unit
clean?   yes _____ no _____

Will it be easy to change the filter?

yes _____ no _____

Has the heat exchanger been tested?

yes _____ no _____

Do any uninsulated **heating ducts** exist in un-
heated spaces?   yes _____ no _____

Are the heating ducts vented properly?

yes _____ no _____

Is there adequate **combustion venting?**

yes _____ no _____

Are the radiators and valves working properly?

yes _____ no _____

Plumbing

Is there copper tubing? _____

galvanized steel? _____

Have you made sure the pipes are *not* made of
lead?   yes _____ no _____

If the pipes are of galvanized steel, do you know
how old they are? _____

Do the water pipes have shut-off valves in the
basement? _____ kitchen? _____
bathroom? _____
Do the waste pipes have leaks in them?
yes _____ no _____
Are the clean-out plugs accessible?
yes _____ no _____
Are they clean? yes _____ no _____
Do they have any leaks in them?
yes _____ no _____
Do you anticipate many plumbing repairs?
yes _____ no _____

Water Heater

Is the water heater **gas** or **electric?**
gas _____ electric _____
What is its **gallon capacity?** _____
Is there a **safety relief valve?** yes _____ no _____
Is there a proper **vent?** yes _____ no _____
Is there a proper **gas supply pipe?**
yes _____ no _____

Crawl Space and Foundation

Are there any signs of **moisture?**
yes _____ no _____
How is the **earth-to-wood clearance?**
good _____ fair _____ poor _____
Is there any evidence of **dry rot?**
yes _____ no _____

Are there any signs of **termites** or **rodents?**
yes _____ no _____
Is the foundation made of continuous concrete?
yes _____ no _____
Are there **piers?** yes _____ no _____
  Are the piers firm? yes _____ no _____
Are the **girders** sagging? yes _____ no _____
  Does the span between the **posts** seem adequate?
  yes _____ no _____
  Is there too much? yes _____ no _____
  Are the **posts** plumb? yes _____ no _____
What is the size of the **floor joists?** _____
  What is their span? _____
  Are they spaced properly? yes _____ no _____
Is there any evidence of a sagging floor?
yes _____ no _____
Is there **bridging** between the joists?
yes _____ no _____
What is the **subfloor** made of? _____
Are there **cracks** in the foundation?
yes _____ no _____
  Are they severe or are they hairline
  cracks? _____

Kitchen

What is the **ceiling** made of? plaster _____
gypsum board _____ plywood _____
other _____

Is the ceiling painted? _____ wallpapered? _____
Is there any evidence of cracks?
    yes _____ no _____
Is there any evidence of a leak?
    yes _____ no _____
What are the **walls** made of?   plaster _____
    gypsum board _____ tile _____ paneling _____
    other _____
Are they painted? _____ wallpapered? _____
Is there any evidence of cracking?
    yes _____ no _____
What are the **floors** made of?   wood _____
    vinyl _____ linoleum _____
Are they carpeted?   yes _____ no _____
    Are they insulated?   yes _____ no _____
What condition are the floors in?
    good _____ fair _____ poor _____
Do you detect a slope in the floor?
    yes _____ no _____
How many **windows** are there? _____
What is the **sash** made of?
    wood _____ metal _____ other _____
    Are the frames in good condition?
    yes _____ no _____
    Are they rotted?   yes _____ no _____
    Are they cracked?   yes _____ no _____
    Are they loose?   yes _____ no _____
    Are they weather-stripped?
    yes _____ no _____

Are the **cords** broken?   yes ____ no ____

Are the **sills** in good condition?

yes ____ no ____

Are they rotted?   yes ____ no ____

Do they show any evidence of air leaks?

yes ____ no ____

Are there **storm windows?**   yes ____ no ____

Are there **screens?**   yes ____ no ____

What is the cost estimate for **plastic sheeting?** _____

Is the **hardware** (locks, knobs, latches, etc.) in good condition?   yes ____ no ____

Will certain items need replacing?

yes ____ no ____

How many? _____

Are the **doors** in good condition?

yes ____ no ____

Do they fit tightly?   yes ____ no ____

Are they weather-stripped?

yes ____ no ____

Do they scrape the floor?   yes ____ no ____

Do they close properly?   yes ____ no ____

Is the doorsill flush?   yes ____ no ____

Are there storm doors?   yes ____ no ____

Are there screen doors?   yes ____ no ____

Are the **plumbing fixtures** in good condition?

yes ____ no ____

Will they need replacement?

yes ____ no ____

Does the faucet drip?   yes ____ no ____

How is the **water pressure?**

strong ____ weak ____

Are there **valves** beneath the sink? ____

Do they leak?   yes ____ no ____

Are there **P trap leaks?**   yes ____ no ____

Is there a **garbage disposal?**   yes ____ no ____

Does it work?   yes ____ no ____

What is the **sink** made of?   stainless steel ____

cast-iron, white ____ steel, white ____

Is it chipped? ____

Is it crazed? ____

Will the sink need replacing? ____

What are the **counter tops** made of?

formica ____ tile ____ wood ____

other ____

What kind of condition are they in?

good ____ fair ____ poor ____

Is there enough **cabinet space?**

yes ____ no ____

Are there enough electrical **outlets?**

yes ____ no ____

What size **wires** are being used?

#12 ____ #14 ____

Are they individually grounded?

yes ____ no ____

What condition are the **light fixtures** in?

good ____ fair ____ poor ____

Will they need replacing?   yes ____ no ____

Is the **stove** gas? ____ electric? ____
   What kind of condition is it in?
   good ____ fair ____ poor ____
   Will it need replacing? yes ____ no ____
   Is there an exhaust fan? yes ____ no ____
Will a **refrigerator** come with the house?
   yes ____ no ____
   If so, is it in operating condition?
   yes ____ no ____

Bathroom

What is the **ceiling** made of? plaster ____
   gypsum board ____ other ____
Are there any cracks in the ceiling?
   yes ____ no ____
What are the **walls** made of? plaster ____
   gypsum board ____ tile ____
   paneling ____
   Are they painted? ____ papered? ____
   What condition are the walls in?
   good ____ fair ____ poor ____
What is the **floor** made of? tile ____
   linoleum ____ vinyl ____ asphalt tile ____
   What condition is the floor in?
   good ____ fair ____ poor ____
Is there an individual shower?
   yes ____ no ____
   Or is the shower in the tub?
   yes ____ no ____

What is the **shower wall** made of?
Formica ____ tile ____ wallboard ____
other ____
What condition are the walls in?
good ____ fair ____ poor ____
If the wall is tiled, what is it tiled with?
mortar ____ mastic ____
What condition is the **grout** in?
good ____ fair ____ poor ____
How is the **water pressure?**
good ____ fair ____ poor ____
What is the **lavatory counter** made of?
tile ____ Formica ____ other ____
What condition is it in?
good ____ fair ____ poor ____
Is the **toilet seal** firm? yes ____ no ____
Or can you detect a leak? yes ____ no ____
Is the **tub** chipped? ____ crazed? ____
serviceable? ____
Are the **fixtures** modern? ____ old? ____
serviceable? ____
Does the **faucet** have a drip? yes ____ no ____
Are there any **P trap leaks?** yes ____ no ____
Are there any **valve leaks?** yes ____ no ____

Living Room

What is the **ceiling** made of? plaster ____
gypsum board ____ Celotex ____
panels ____ other ____

Are there cracks in the ceiling?

yes _____ no _____

Is there any evidence of leaks?

yes _____ no _____

What are the **walls** made of?   plaster _____

gypsum board _____ paneling _____

other _____

Are there any cracks in the walls?

yes _____ no _____

What are the **floors** made of?   hardwood _____

fir _____ asphalt tile _____ wall-to-wall _____

other _____

What condition are the floors in?

good _____ fair _____ poor _____

Is there a slope to the floor?   yes _____ no _____

Do the **doors** fit properly?   yes _____ no _____

Are the locks on the doors secure?

yes _____ no _____

Are the doors weather-stripped?

yes _____ no _____

Is the doorsill flush?   yes _____ no _____

How many **windows** are there? _____

Are the windows framed in wood? _____

metal? _____ other? _____

Are any windows cracked?   yes _____ no _____

Are the **frames** rotted?   yes _____ no _____

Are there any air leaks?   yes _____ no _____

Are the windows weather-stripped?

yes _____ no _____

Are the sills rotted?   yes ____   no ____

Are there any air leaks in the **sills?**
yes ____   no ____

Are there **storm windows?**   yes ____   no ____

What is the cost estimate for **plastic
sheeting?** _____

What is the **sash** made of?
aluminum ____   wood ____

Is there any evidence of **leakage?**
yes ____   no ____

If there is a **fireplace,** does it have a damper?
yes ____   no ____

What is the condition of the bricks?
good ____   fair ____   poor ____

Is the grout firm?   yes ____   no ____

Is the mantel level?   yes ____   no ____

Is there any evidence of smoke?
yes ____   no ____

How many **heat registers** are there? _____

How many **electric outlets** are there? _____

Smoke Detectors

How many **smoke detectors** are there? _____

Are they working properly?   yes ____   no ____

Are they conveniently located (near bedrooms, in
the hallways, etc.)?   yes ____   no ____

Have they been placed too close to areas prone to
harmless smoke (stoves, laundry rooms)?
yes ____   no ____

Family Room

What is the **ceiling** made of?   plaster ____
gypsum board ____ Celotex ____
panels ____ other ____

Are there cracks in the ceiling?
yes ____ no ____

Is there any evidence of leaks?
yes ____ no ____

What are the **walls** made of?   plaster ____
gypsum board ____ paneling ____
other ____

Are there any cracks in the walls?
yes ____ no ____

What are the **floors** made of?   hardwood ____
fir ____ asphalt tile ____ wall-to-wall ____
other ____

What condition are the floors in?
good ____ fair ____ poor ____

Is there a slope to the floor?   yes ____ no ____

Do the **doors** fit properly?   yes ____ no ____

Are the locks on the doors secure?
yes ____ no ____

Are the doors weather-stripped?
yes ____ no ____

Is the doorsill flush?   yes ____ no ____

How many **windows** are there?   _____

Are the windows framed in wood?   ____
metal? ____ other? ____

Are any windows cracked?   yes ____ no ____

Are the **frames** rotted?   yes ____   no ____
Are there any air leaks?   yes ____   no ____
Are the windows weather-stripped?
yes ____   no ____
Are the sills rotted?   yes ____   no ____
Are there any air leaks in the **sills?**
yes ____   no ____
Are there **storm windows?**   yes ____   no ____
What is the cost estimate for **plastic
   sheeting?** _____
What is the **sash** made of?
aluminum ____   wood ____
Is there any evidence of **leakage?**
yes ____   no ____
If there is a **fireplace,** does it have a damper?
   yes ____   no ____
What is the condition of the bricks?
good ____   fair ____   poor ____
Is the grout firm?   yes ____   no ____
Is the mantcl level?   yes ____   no ____
Is there any evidence of smoke?
yes ____   no ____
How many **heat registers** are there? _____
How many **electric outlets** are there? _____

Bedroom

What is the **ceiling** made of?   plaster ____
   gypsum board ____   Celotex ____
   panels ____   other ____

Are there cracks in the ceiling?

yes _____ no _____

Is there any evidence of leaks?

yes _____ no _____

What are the **walls** made of?   plaster _____
gypsum board _____ paneling _____
other _____

Are there any cracks in the walls?

yes _____ no _____

What are the **floors** made of?   hardwood _____
fir _____ asphalt tile _____ wall-to-wall _____
other _____

What condition are the floors in?

good _____ fair _____ poor _____

Is there a slope to the floor?   yes _____ no _____

Do the **doors** fit properly?   yes _____ no _____

Are the locks on the door secure?

yes _____ no _____

Are the doors weather-stripped?

yes _____ no _____

Is the doorsill flush?   yes _____ no _____

How many **windows** are there?   _____

Are the windows framed in wood? _____
metal? _____ other? _____

Are any windows cracked?   yes _____ no _____

Are the **frames** rotted?   yes _____ no

Are there any air leaks?   yes _____ no _____

Are the windows weather-stripped?

yes _____ no _____

Are the sills rotted?   yes _____ no _____

Are there any air leaks in the **sills?**

yes _____ no _____

Are there **storm windows?**   yes _____ no _____

What is the cost estimate for **plastic sheeting?** _____

What is the **sash** made of?

aluminum _____ wood _____

Is there any evidence of **leakage?**

yes _____ no _____

If there is a **fireplace,** does it have a damper?

yes _____ no _____

What is the condition of the bricks?

good _____ fair _____ poor _____

Is the grout firm?   yes _____ no _____

Is the mantel level?   yes _____ no _____

Is there any evidence of smoke?

yes _____ no _____

How many **heat registers** are there? _____

How many **electric outlets** are there? _____

Glossary

Amp   Ampere. Measurement of electricity. Equal to the movement of 6.28 quintillion electrons per second.

Angle of repose   Poetic but accurate phrase. The slope at which the earth is at rest. Natural slope.

Angle stop valve   Shut-off valves beneath sinks, lavatories, and toilets.

Appraised value   Market value. An amount the assessor thinks the property is worth.

Assessed value   A percentage of appraised value for tax purposes. It's confusing and meant to be. If it were clear, the common people could understand it. The tax rate is a certain amount for each one hundred dollars of assessed value.

Bearing wall   Supports a floor above, or a portion of the roof. See Curtain wall.

Blistering paint   Film of paint separated from its surface. Usually caused by moisture in the wood.

Bonnet packing   Pliable material around a valve stem to prevent water from leaking around the handle. If you can't find the right size packing, use cotton string.

BTU   British thermal unit. Amount of heat required to raise a pound of water one degree Fahrenheit. Very close to the amount of heat from a wooden kitchen match.

164

Built-up roof   Same as tar-and-gravel roof. Several layers of thin tar paper with hot tar between courses, gravel on top.

Buttress   A support projecting from a wall.

Butyl   A plastic caulking compound.

Calignum   Liquid plastic used to fill the pores of deteriorated wood, especially rotted areas. Excellent for minor wood rot around windows. Other brand names: Git-Rot, Rot-Cure.

Carpenter ants   Large ants that live in hollowed spaces in wood. More a nuisance than a destroyer. Cleanliness is the answer.

Casing   The wooden boards of various width on the wall outlining windows and doors.

Cats   Usually two-by-fours nailed between studs halfway between floor and ceiling. See Fire stop.

Caulking   Any substance used to fill cracks.

Cellulose debris   Termite inspectors' favorite phrase to mystify homeowners. Not a serious house disease. It's wood scraps lying on the earth beneath a house and not attached to the structure.

Cement   A fine powder made from limestone, shale, marl, gypsum, and other rock products. These materials are fired in a large kiln, then ground to a gray powder. That's cement. When mixed with water, sand, and rocks, it makes concrete.

Centrally located   To what? A football stadium, an auditorium, a cemetery? A suspect real estate term.

Chalking   Powdering of oil-based paint after a few years. It's a self-cleaning process to be expected.

Checking   Paint film that looks like alligator hide. Generally caused by poor primer.

Cheerful   Real estate term. Probably means that the seller is going to be laughing all the way to the bank.

Circuit   A complete path of electric current through

several outlets, lights, or switches and returning to the source, which is the fuse box or circuit breaker box.

Circuit breaker   Safety device to interrupt a circuit. It takes the place of fuses, which were just as good.

Clean-outs   Plugs or caps in sewer line easily removed to clean the pipe when necessary.

Clearance   If pest control inspector reports that a house is free of wood-destroying organisms he issues a clearance. The house meets pest control specifications.

Closing costs   A charge based on percentage of the loan. Please pay the loan company.

Cold air return   Large ducts that lead cold air, or return air, to a furnace. Absolutely necessary.

Collar beam   Beam, usually made of wood, used to connect opposite rafters together. Sometimes called straining piece.

Combustion venting   Necessary fresh air leading to an oil- or gas-burning appliance. Without fresh air, the flame burns less efficiently. Same as oxygen venting.

Concrete   A mixture of cement, sand, water, and rocks.

Condensation   Moisture forming on a cold surface where warmer air strikes. Windows and metal sash make good conditions for condensation. See Dew point.

Contingency   Dependent on something, a condition. "I'll buy this house if it checks out to suit me." You have made an offer contingent upon a favorable inspection. Good for you.

Crawl space   The area between the earth and the floor. Not the most inviting area but an important one. Get acquainted with it.

Cricket   A built-up structure, six or eight inches high, usually metal, between a fireplace chimney and the upslope of the roof to prevent water and debris from gathering in the cavity.

Cripple   A short wall stud to support headers, lintels, window plates, roof rafters.

Cross-bracing   One-by-three pieces of board criss-crossed to support the floor joists. Usually they are placed ten to twelve feet apart.

Curtain wall   A partition that does not support an overhead ceiling or roof. Same as nonbearing wall.

d (penny)   L. *denarius*. A small coin. The symbol now signifies the length of nails: 8d, 2½-inches long; 16d, 3½ inches; etc. Ask for 8-penny nails.

Damp-wood termites   Zootermopsis. The largest termite. Lives primarily on dead and decaying wood. Needs much moisture. Fix that leaky shower or toilet.

Damper   A piece of metal in a pipe or flue to control the passage of heat.

Darby   A wide board used to smooth concrete.

Decorator's dream   More likely a nightmare. Real estate term.

Deed or grant deed   A legal document stating ownership of property. The document proves you have title to the property.

Dew point   The temperature at which moisture forms on a wall or substance. Warm air contains moisture. When it strikes a cold wall the moisture is wrung out; it condenses. The temperature that causes moisture to condense is the dew point temperature.

Diagonal bracing   Lumber or steel on a wall at an angle to the vertical side. Not to prevent tipping (that's buttress bracing). See Gusset.

Dieldrin   A poisonous powder for killing wood-destroying insects.

Dielectric union   Sometimes called insulated union. A nonconducting plumbing fitting used to join pipes made of two different materials to prevent electrolysis.

Differential separation   Won't line up. One side of a crack is separated to a different level than the other side, or dropped to a different position.

Doll house   Probably what it says. Small, cramped, and overpriced. A real estate term.

Door jamb   See Jamb.

Down spouts   Vertical pipes from gutters. Also called leader pipes. Use them. The more you control water, the better the house.

Drain tile   Pipe used to collect and remove water from earth.

Drip edge   Thin metal edging installed on eaves and rakes to protect the wood from moisture.

Dry rot   Fungus that destroys wood. A misnomer. Should be wood rot.

Dry wall   Interior wall or ceiling covering; usually gypsum board. Has no water in it, unlike plaster.

Dry-wood termites   Kalotermes. Termites that live in wood. Often found in attics.

Ducts   Pipes or passageways through which warm air is distributed from the heating plant.

Eaves   The portion of a roof that extends beyond the wall.

Efflorescence   Literally means flowering. A white powdery hydrate that forms on concrete or masonry when moisture is present. The moisture may be behind the wall.

Elbow   An ell. A fitting that makes a turn in a pipe.

Electronic filters   Sometimes called electrostatic air cleaners. A super filter that has electrically charged plates. They'll pick up dust and pollen that go through ordinary filters. Good for sufferers of allergies.

Escrow "Holder of the stakes." Money held by a company to pay various people or agencies per instructions.

Fascia The board covering the end of roof rafters at the eave line.

Fire stop Solid blocking between wall studs halfway up a wall. Their purpose is to reduce oxygen in case of fire.

Firebricks Special bricks that can take high temperatures. Used in the firebox area of fireplaces.

Fireclay A mixture of clay, sand, and cement. Mixed with water, it is used as grout between fireplace bricks in the firebox area.

Flashing Tar paper or metal used for waterproofing where walls and roof meet, or around windows, chimneys, vents, and valleys.

Flue A pipe or chamber to carry gases; a chimney. You'll get sick if you have a faulty one.

Footing The bottom portion of a foundation. The footing is usually wider than the foundation for better weight distribution.

Forced-air furnace A furnace that forces heat through ducts by a fan and motor.

Foreclosure Legal proceeding in which a loan company takes back the house when payments have not been met.

Foundation Whatever supports the house that is in contact with earth. Concrete is best. If concrete, the foundation includes the footing.

Full disclosure Any fault known by seller must be revealed. Agents must inform buyer if he or she knows of such faults.

Fungicide A poison used to kill or retard growth of fungus. It's poisonous to other things too, so be careful.

Fungus   For our purposes fungus is a mold that destroys wood. It has to have moisture to grow, so beware.

Furring   Strips of lumber used as a base to bring a wall out to a desired position. If a wall is uneven, or a pipe projects too far, you fur out to get beyond the highest portion, then add the finishing material.

Gable   The portion of a roof that goes from the eave line to the ridge or top in an unbroken plane. It has to go back down again to make a true gable. That makes the roof double-sloped.

Girder   Beam. Usually wood, to support loads without close vertical posts. Generally beneath floors.

Glue lam   Laminated wooden beam made up of several pieces of wood glued together.

Grade   Earth level. In termite parlance, earth and grade are the same thing.

Gravity furnace   Heat rises through ducts without a fan. No motor, no filter. Good system.

Ground fault interrupter (GFI)   A safety device that monitors the difference between current flowing through the hot and neutral wire. If there is an imbalance of current greater than five milliamps, the current will be cut off instantly. The GFI measures for electric current leakage.

Grout   The visible mortar between joints of tile or bricks. It is often colored to blend or contrast with tile.

Gusset   Literally, armpit. In building, it's a triangular plywood brace secured at post and beam joints to prevent side movement.

Gypsum board   "Sheetrock," or dry wall.

Hairline crack   Minor cracks, caused from shrinking or slight house movement.

Header   Lumber spanning door or window opening. Same as lintel.

Hearth   The portion of a fireplace on which the fire is built. It often extends into the room, level with the base of the firebox.

Heat exchanger   The metal surrounding the burners in a furnace. Sometimes called a firebox.

Hip   In building it is a type of roof that has four surfaces; the ends are triangles, the other two sides slope up to the gable, making truncated triangles.

Homestead   A home or property protected by law against certain debts. The old meaning of "homestead" is not used much any more. Check into homesteading your house.

Horsefeathers   Long, thin strips of wood, wedge-shaped, to lay along the ends of a shingle or shake roof to smooth it out before applying asphalt shingles.

Hydronic furnace   Forced hot-water heating.

Individual grounding   An electrical outlet that has a third wire, which connects to a ground device.

Insulated union   See Dielectric union.

Insulated windows   Two or more panes of glass with a dead-air space between each.

Insulation   Everybody knows what insulation is. See R-value.

Interceptor drain   A ditch cut into a hillside on an angle to collect water and direct it away from your house.

Jack rafters   Short rafters that extend from wall plates to hip or valley rafters.

Jack studs   Short studs beneath window plates.

Jamb   The wood framing on either side of a door.

Joist   Lumber laid on edge to support floor or ceiling.

Leader pipe   Vertical pipe leading from gutters. Also called downspouts.

Lintel   See Header.

Mantel   A shelf above the fireplace on which to set clocks or various dust collectors. Used seasonally to display Christmas cards.

Mastic   Glue or paste. Used for cementing tile, linoleum, wood, or wood products.

Mineral deposits   Impurities in water and rust from steel pipes that forms on interior of water pipes. This can be hastened by electrolysis. Use insulated unions.

Molding   Finish wood in various shapes used for decorative purposes and to hide mistakes. "Cover it up with molding."

Mortgage   A written instrument showing that certain property has been used as security for loan of money. They're okay when you need them but make the happiest fire when returned.

Mud   Concrete mortar. Base for installing ceramic tile in showers.

Mullion   The vertical divider between window or door glass.

Muntins   I doubt you'll need this word, but just in case: they divide the glass into smaller panes.

Nonbearing wall   See Curtain wall.

Nosing   Metal strip around the edge of the roof.

Obligated room   Real estate term. A room that you have to go through to get to another room.

Outlet   Convenience outlet, electrical receptacle. Plug a cord in, hope it works.

Oxygen venting   See Combustion venting.

P trap   That part of the drain beneath a sink that turns up, then meets another pipe that goes through the wall. The "P" is the lowest portion of pipe. It holds water all the time to prevent sewer gases from entering the house.

Peeling paint   Thin film of paint loosening from surface. Usually caused by moisture within the wall.

Penny   See *d.*

Penta   Pentachlorophenol wood preservative. Good against termites and fungus. Sounds like a panacea but isn't.

Perimeter foundation   The outside wall of the house; this is what the house rests on.

Pier   Concrete base to support posts and keep them off the earth.

Pitch   In our terms it's two things that will help you keep in tune with building. One: slope. Usually referred to as the incline of a roof. Two: the messy resin from conifers such as fir and pine trees.

Plenum   Literally: full. The large metal box attached to furnace from which heating ducts emerge.

Plumb   Vertical.

Points   In the financial world it means 1 to 1½ percent of the amount loaned on the property. Lenders use it for additional funds.

Polyurethane   Plastic insulating board. One of the best.

Powder-post beetle.   No friend of antiques. A small beetle that lives in wood. They literally turn the wood to powder. Floor joists they love.

R-value   Resistance value. A figure used to signify the insulating value per inch of a product. The higher the R-value, the better the insulation.

Rabbet   A groove cut out of the edge or the face of lumber. Usually rectangular.

Radiant heat   The way sunshine heats; it emits heat

rays. Heat in a floor or ceiling emits heat to the room. It may be from hot water or electricity.

Rafters   The sloping timber of a roof to which the roof surface is nailed.

Rail   The top and bottom horizontal wood members in a door; attached to stiles, which are the vertical members. Also the top and bottom of a stairway, the handrail.

Rake   The edge of a roof opposite the eaves. Usually over an end wall.

Ridge   The highest point of a gabled or hip roof. Ridge pole is the timber on which the rafters rest on a gabled roof.

Rise   The height of a step.

Riser   The vertical board at the toe end of each step.

Romex   A type of electric wire. Most commonly used wire in houses. Sometimes called nonmetallic sheathed cable.

Rust buildup   Particles of rust that form on the inside of steel plumbing pipes. Eventually there is more rust than opening.

Rustic   Usually raw, unpainted exterior. Could be interior. Often referred to as quaint.

Screeds   A guide. Boards placed in position at a level to which concrete is laid. A straight edge reaches from one screed to another and scrapes concrete to level of screeds.

Second mortgage   When a buyer hasn't enough money to pay for a house, either by loan or his or her own cash, a second loan, usually small, is made from some other source. Interest is higher than first mortgage.

Service panel   Main electric box on house where electric wire from street is connected.

Shake   A shingle split from a piece of log usually three or four feet long.

Shear strength The dictionary says tangential movement, which is preventing movement on a plane, such as a floor. You don't want your floor to move from side to side. Give it shear strength and it won't.

Sheathing Exterior wall or roof covering. Wall sheathing is often covered by a finish product, like stucco.

Sheetrock (trademark) Sometimes called dry wall or gypsum board. Two pieces of paper with gypsum between. Various thicknesses.

Shoe A quarter round piece of molding set against the corner where wall meets floor. It goes on top of the finish floor against the baseboard.

Sill Sill plate. A wood member attached to foundation on which the structure is built.

Sleeper A wood member sometimes embedded in a concrete slab or laid on the surface, to which the subfloor is attached.

Soffit Specifically, the underside of an architectural feature such as a beam, arch, cornice, etc. The common reference is to the underside of the eaves which have been covered with a finishing material.

Square Roofers use the term most. A square is 100 square feet.

Stabilize To support. To stop or arrest settling or movement.

Stain A liquid that penetrates wood; usually oil-based.

Stile The vertical wood members in a door; attached to the rails.

Stringer The sides of stairs on which the treads rest.

Strongback A wood member in an attic area, stretching from one supporting wall to another. Ceiling joists are attached to the strongback to prevent sagging.

Structural fault A threatening weakness in construction.

Stucco An exterior wall finish. Composed of cement, sand, lime, and water.

Studs   Vertical members in a wall to which interior and exterior covering are nailed.

Subterranean termites   Reticulitermes. Small gray insects, ¼ inch long. Live in earth but feed on wood. Do not expose themselves to air. Reach wood by self-made tubes or by earth-to-wood contact.

Summer switch   A switch on a forced-air furnace to operate the fan manually with no heat. A good idea on a hot day.

Sweetheart arrangement   A payoff. "As long as you cooperate, I'll give you jobs. But don't forget my percentage."

Termiticide   An antitermite substance. Pentachlorophenol or chlordane.

Thermocouple   A safety device on most gas- or oil-fired appliances that shuts off the supply of fuel if the pilot light blows out. Commonly found on furnaces and water heaters.

Thermopane   One or more panes of glass with vacuum between. Difficult to replace broken glass; you can't suck that hard. Excellent insulation.

Thermostat   A mechanism to control heat automatically.

Threshold   The bottom of a doorway on which you step or tread to enter or exit.

Title insurance   Insurance on property against claim of ownership by an unknown heir or creditor. A one-time cost. Lasts as long as you own the property.

Toenail   A nail on a slant through one member to another.

Toilet seal   A ring of putty or wax between the toilet and the floor. Don't try to get along without it.

Tread   Stair steps.

Trim   Finish material, such as molding. It can cover many sins.

Valley   It's the V on roofs where an inside or convex change in roof direction is made. The best valleys have metal in the V.

Vapor barrier   A waterproof covering to prevent moisture penetration. Used on walls and beneath concrete slabs.

Veneer   To cover up. Generally it's thin pieces of good wood covering a cheap or poor surface. Brick veneer is genuine, but the bricks are a covering, not bearing.

Vent   A pipe to carry either foul air from an area or fresh air to an area. A furnace vent pipe carries exhaust fumes away.

Volts   Electric power. The more speed at which electrons travel, the more electric power (230 volts is more powerful than 115 volts).

Watts   The amount of power flowing through a wire. Volts (speed) multiplied by amps equal watts.

Weather-stripping   Material added to door or window frames to prevent passage of air through tiny cracks.

Wood rot   Same as dry rot, only a more accurate phrase. Both to be avoided. Deterioration of wood due to growth of fungus. Fungus requires moisture to grow.

Bibliography

Government publications, federal and state, can be obtained from the U.S. Department of Agriculture Extension Office in the city nearest to you.

Basic Housing Inspection. Public Health Service. Publication no. 2123. Superintendent of Documents, U.S. Government Printing Office, Washington, D.C.

Carpentry and Building Construction. U.S. Army TM 5–460. Superintendent of Documents, U.S. Government Printing Office, Washington, D.C.

Condensation Problems in Your House. U.S. Department of Agriculture, Forest Service. Publication no. 373. Superintendent of Documents, Washington, D.C.

Finding and Keeping a Healthy House. U.S. Department of Agriculture, Forest Service. Publication no. 1284 (Termites).

Remodelers' Handbook. Craftsman Book Co., 542 Stevens Ave., Solano Beach, Ca. 92075.

H. P. Richter. *Wiring Simplified.* Park Publishing, Box 5527, Lake St. Station, Minneapolis, Minn. 55408.

Rex Roberts. *Your Engineered House.* J. B. Lippincott Co., Philadelphia, Pa. 19105.

Wise Home Buying. U.S. Department of Housing and Urban Development. Washington, D.C.

Wood Decay in Houses: How to Prevent and Control It. U.S.

Department of Agriculture, Home and Garden Bulletin no. 73.

Peter Yenev. *Peace of Mind in Earthquake Country.* Chronicle Books, San Francisco, Ca. 94102.

Index

About the Author

The late George Hoffman *spent thirty years learning, teaching, helping. In 1948 he moved to Sausalito and began to learn about house-building by reading, observing, then working with a contractor, and finally by building his own house from the ground up—foundations, construction, plumbing, electricity, roof, and all the myriad extras that crop up as one goes along. The house was built on a small lot 400 yards from an abandoned shipyard. His career as a recycler began with the use of the many materials left in this yard, in the city dump, in old buildings—all the discards of an affluent society. Later he built another house entirely by himself, and then went into remodeling.*

When friends asked him to look over houses before they bought, he realized he had a valuable and helpful business before him. This business grew solely by word of mouth. By 1965, he had examined more than 3,500 houses, both for prospective buyers and for owners anxious to keep their property in tip-top shape. He took the buyer or owner with him, diagnosing and explaining the house as he inspected. George Hoffman also taught home inspection in an adult education course at the College of Marin. He was a frequent guest on radio, answering questions about houses, and often gave talks on home inspection and maintenance, both of vital interest to buyers and owners in these inflationary times.